Under a Shared Umbrella

Tales of Synchronicity and Happenstance

Bobbi Zehner and Kate Conklin Corcoran, editors

ISBN: 1495248933
ISBN 13: 9781495248931
Library of Congress Control Number: 2014917228
CreateSpace Independent Publishing Platform
North Charleston, South Carolina

Acknowledgements

We would like to acknowledge our many contributors, *the connectors,* whose willingness to share their stories made this book a reality.

A special thank you to Rae Welch for his cover illustration.

For their constant support, encouragement, and love, we are grateful to Larry Zehner and Marty Corcoran.

We dedicate this book to our mothers, Ardell Nickels and Dolores Kozla Conklin, whose genuine love of and interest in people created those same traits in each of us.

Table of Contents

Chapter One

I believe in an everyday sort of magic--the inexplicable connected-
ness we sometimes experience with places, people, works of art and
the like; the eerie appropriateness of moments of synchronicity.
--Charles de Lint

Chapter Two

There is no such thing as chance; and what seems to us merest accident springs from the deepest source of destiny.
-- Frederick Schiller (1759-1805)

Chapter Three

A small change of circumstances here or there and our ships would no doubt have passed in the night.
--Robert Wood

Chapter Four

Is there something about the way we form personal connections that heightens the likelihood of synchronicities?
--Carolyn Zahn-Waxler

Chapter Five

Friendships link and loop and interweave until they mesh the world.
-- Pam Brown

Chapter Six

How many times do people come into our lives without being aware
that we have mutual connections? Perhaps that's partly why our skin
tingles in moments like these, realizing that we could just as easily
never have made the discovery.
-- Bobbi Zehner

Chapter Seven

Synchronicity is an ever present reality for those who have eyes to see.
-- Carl Jung

Chapter Eight

The afternoon knows what the morning never suspected.
-- Swedish Proverb

Chapter Nine

Our lives are connected by a thousand invisible threads.
-- Herman Melville

Chapter Ten

Every person is a new door to a different world.
-- David Mamet, *Six Degrees of Separation*

Introduction

You are sitting at a sidewalk café in Paris when an unknown woman approaches and asks, "Aren't you Bobbi, from Chicago?"

You are attending the wedding of a cousin-by-marriage and discover that the groom is your next-door playmate from 25 years ago.

Or perhaps you are in line at a Haagen-Dazs ice cream stand at a temple in Thailand, when you hear your name being called.

Has anything like this ever happened to you? For example, you are on holiday in Holland and pass your next-door neighbor from the U.S. on a street in Amsterdam. Do not such chance encounters defy probability? The stories in this anthology support the existence of such improbabilities. In *Under a Shared Umbrella: Tales of Synchronicity and Happenstance*, people from throughout the United States, as well as from Australia, England, France and South Africa, share their tales of synchronicity and happenstance. In some cases, they have written their own stories; others agreed to be interviewed, but asked us to do the actual writing. A few preferred to be anonymous, and we honored that request.

The tales selected are those that we felt would conjure recognition, fascination and a joy akin to our own—stories that raise the possibility that all life is connected, as in Carl's Jung's "unus mundus": one world. The catalyst for the title, *Under a Shared Umbrella*, is our first story, "Fewer Than Six Degrees of Separation," in which Bobbi is sitting at that sidewalk café in Paris, under what becomes the first shared umbrella.

As we began work on this book, we also sought an umbrella term for these stories. More than coincidence, more than happenstance, often fewer than six degrees of separation, what we were gathering were stories of synchronicity. Psychotherapist Carl G. Jung (1875–1961) was largely responsible for pioneering the concept of synchronicity, which he defined as "meaningful coincidence":

What I found were "coincidences" which were connected so meaningfully that their "chance" occurrence would represent a degree of improbability that would have to be represented by an astronomical figure. (Jung, *Synchronicity: an Acausal Connecting Principle,* 1952).

Scholars still explore and debate the theory. Self-help gurus mine the concept for ways to improve life, but our purpose here is simpler. For the stories in *Under a Shared Umbrella,* synchronicity refers to the coming together of people, in the exact same place at the exact same time, in a situation that is meaningful for them, without a deliberate cause, and unforeseen by any of the parties.

We call our contributors "connectors." Connectors tend to be outgoing people with a deep, genuine interest in and curiosity about others. Rather than simply making small talk, connectors ask probing questions and pursue their answers. Connectors are also more likely to look beyond accepted beliefs, mores, and paradigms, so that they notice what might go unseen by others.

Many connectors are travelers. Visiting other places, of course, provides opportunity to meet more people who may have a connection in some way. Too, travelers tend to strike up longer and deeper conversations because they are away from home and curious about the people they encounter. Carl Jung's concept of synchronicity had its roots in his work with the unconscious and with parapsychology; several of our contributors have had unexplainable spiritual experiences. And some people just appeared at the right place at the right time. As Carolyn Stiegler writes, "I often wonder how many people have just turned the corner before I got there."

We have our own tale to tell. One warm summer night, we each happened to be at Madison's Memorial Union Terrace. With Bobbi were two friends: Bonnie from Madison and Kathy from Chicago.

Kate and Bobbi recognized each other from local teacher union meetings, but Bonnie was the mutual friend, the connector. When Kate mentioned that she was originally from Chicago, Kathy connected Kate's last name with that of her friend Patty, asking if they were related. Yes, Patty happened to be Kate's sister. The same Patty Conklin who played on Kathy's Chicago softball team. Another connection through a chance meeting: one which led to Bobbi and Kate becoming close friends. Then one day, while beneath a shared umbrella at Michael's Frozen Custard, we decided to write this book. We have imagined gathering with all of our authors under a café umbrella. The thrill that accompanies a story to which we can each relate, however, is not imaginary: it is deliciously real. May you, too, experience that thrill.

Bobbi Zehner and Kate Conklin Corcoran

Fewer than Six Degrees of Separation
Bobbi Zehner

While sitting in a sidewalk cafe in 1972, watching people stroll along Les Champs-Elysées, I was approached by a young woman from amid the meandering crowd. "Excuse me, but aren't you Bobbi from Chicago?" She added, "Bobbi from O'Leary's?"

Stunned, I scanned the boulevard for Allen Funt of television's "Candid Camera" fame, or at least a face I might recognize. I saw neither.

Mary Sheehan, the young woman standing before me, had just arrived from Venice. Her original plan had been to visit a brother studying at The Sorbonne. At the last minute, the brother cabled Mary, instructing her to stay home; he was returning to the U.S. Undaunted, Mary chose to travel around Europe alone.

I had just hitchhiked from Amsterdam--an experience I wouldn't advise today-- and was relishing a Parisian pastry, when Mary approached. She recognized me, she said, because "Your friends in O'Leary's were giving you a royal sendoff and I happened to be in the bar at the time." What are the odds of spotting a familiar face, seen only once before, while traveling abroad? Appreciating the uniqueness of the moment, I invited Mary to join me for a glass of wine.

We compared travel notes, talked at length about our Chicago lives and shared more than a few laughs. "Would you like to try to get into The Moulin Rouge this evening?" I asked.

"Absolutement!" said Mary.

Dining at the infamous cabaret would have been exorbitant; well beyond our means. But we discovered that for the price of a drink apiece, we could watch the entire floor show, while standing at the back bar of The Moulin Rouge. Neither of us had ever seen live burlesque theater. We were awed by the impeccable timing of jugglers with flaming batons and the precision of titillating cancan dancers. The outrageous act of a bawdy mime left our cheeks flushed, as we departed to go our separate ways.

The next day I took the Hovercraft to the White Cliffs of Dover from Calais, confident that Mary and I would see each other once we were stateside. Because of that one chance encounter, Mary and I returned to Chicago as kindred spirits. In and out of O'Leary's, we often talked about traveling together in the future, with an eye toward Spain.

About a year later, Mary suggested we take a cruise. "What? I thought we were going to Spain!" I balked at Mary's suggestion, convinced that only old folks took cruises. This was before the launch of "Love Boat"--the long-running television series in which passengers and crew members weekly dabbled in romance and adventure. However, Mary campaigned enthusiastically and I eventually relented, sure that I was betraying my own better judgment. Passage was booked, and another O'Leary's sendoff went into motion.

Joining the celebration, Jeannie, a friend originally from England, asked which line we would be sailing. "Cunard," Mary and I responded in unison.

"Which ship?"

When we told her, Jeannie beamed. Coincidentally, and in far fewer than the popular six degrees of separation, her father had been the captain of that very ship when she was still a youngster. How fitting that we should cruise the Caribbean aboard a ship, aptly named *The Adventurer*, once captained by Jeannie's father.

The next day Mary and I flew to San Juan, where we stood in a long line snaking around itself on the dock. I heard my name being called, and a young woman came toward me. With a proper British accent, she said, "Hello, I'm Helen, the ship's photographer. Your friend Jeannie happens to be my dear friend and childhood mate from Bournemouth." This time I wasn't the only one stunned, as Mary's jaw dropped open, too.

We were grateful when Helen plucked us from the waiting line and led us to our cabin. A surprise bottle of champagne greeted us with this note: "Just let Helen see to your Bon Voyage. You're in very good hands! Love, Jeannie." What a welcome!

That one serendipitous meeting in Paris set my course for more than a cruise with Mary Sheehan, in 1973. It put me on a lifelong path of travel filled with curiosity and awe. Helen Keller, a role model for all ages, said, "Life is a daring adventure or nothing." How can my attitude be any less?

Chapter One

I believe in an everyday sort of magic--the inexplicable connected-ness we sometimes experience with places, people, works of art and the like; the eerie appropriateness of moments of synchronicity.

Charles de Lint

A Photographic Memory
Sherry Brenner

I lived in and moved from numerous places in my early married years. As a result, I had collected, and eventually lost track of, lots of friends during that period. One friend was Marilyn. She and John had befriended my husband and me during the year we lived in Lake Geneva, Wisconsin. We had known them for six or more years when we were all living in Hawaii. Marilyn was a sweet lady, mother of three kids, plumpish, with the complexion of a peach. We saw a lot of each other, as our husbands taught at the same college prep academy in Kamuela on the Big Island. Our teaching community was very close. We were all young, had left families behind on the mainland, and were starting new families. We ate in the same dining hall and spent a lot of recreational hours together. It was very hard when my husband and I eventually left our little close-knit group for the mainland. I knew we wouldn't see these very special people again.

After a number of moves and a divorce, perhaps ten years after leaving Hawaii, I ended up in Madison, Wisconsin. I can't recall the circumstances, but somehow I was offered a free portrait at a photo studio at Madison's East Towne Mall. As I was waiting to be called for my sitting, my eyes wandered around the studio to the portraits on the wall. At the sight of one of them, I did a double-take. And then another. The people in this portrait looked very familiar: a father, a very sweet-looking mother, and three teen-aged children. Could they possibly be my old friends from Hawaii? It had been a long time since I had seen them, but these people sure looked familiar.

I wondered if the studio would be allowed to tell me the names and perhaps the phone numbers of these people. Probably not: respect for privacy and all that. Bummer! I looked at the portrait again and mentally sent my old friends my warmest regards.

Every once in a while, the world graces us with a wondrous surprise and we feel the oneness of the universe. Marilyn, having driven down from her home in nearby Beaver Dam to pick up her portraits, walked through the studio door at that very moment--still sweet and plump-ish with the complexion of a peach. Yes, we did recognize each other immediately: "Is that really you?" And we laughed delightedly at such an amazing coincidence, falling into each other's arms with a swoop.

Meriter Hospital's Volunteer
Bobbi Zehner

April of '03 found me sitting, nervous and worried, in a deserted hall-way at Meriter Hospital. Next to me sat the volunteer who had just transported a seriously ill Larry into the CAT scan room. Trying to pass the time, I struck up a conversation with the young man, whose hospital ID tagged him simply as Michael.

"So, Michael, do you plan to become a doctor some day? Is that why you volunteer here?"

"No, but I might go to nursing school back home, after I gradu-ate," he politely responded.

"That would be nice. Where is home?"

"Chicago."

"The Chicagoland area?"

"No, Chicago."

"I'm from Chicago. In fact, my brother is still there. He lives at Lincoln and Irving."

Michael's eyes grew wide, as he sputtered, "I live at Lincoln and Irving!"

"Well, my brother actually lives on Byron."

"*I* live on Byron!" Michael almost shouted.

It was then that I flashed on an "Aha" moment from a few years earlier, when I learned that my brother had moved to the same Chicago street as my old chum Michael Holland. I looked for a last name on the young man's ID tag. There wasn't one. Even though I had never met him before, I recognized his mother in his eyes. I chided, "MICHAEL HOLLAND! You were supposed to call me when you arrived in Madison!"

"How do you know my name?" he gasped.

This is the point where I wish I had said, "Because I'm clairvoyant!" Instead, I explained the connection and was not at all surprised when his dad phoned me that very same night!

After the Snow
Kate Conklin Corcoran

What we are calling synchronicity, another friend calls "the road taken." Going to a new store, traveling on a different road, leaving the house a few minutes earlier or later than planned, car accidents, snowstorms—any number of things can combine to create synchronicity. On December 27, 2009, all of these factors came together in Des Plaines, Illinois.

On December 26, 2009, a major snowfall hit the Chicago area, concentrated especially in the northwest suburbs. The next day, the snow had ended, but ice covered everything. The roads were treacherous, and cars spinning out of control became routine by early afternoon. Jackie and Bill's ninth-grade son was on his way to a wrestling meet. The parent driving the boys to the meet was one of the drivers who had spun out of control, eventually hitting a tree. Everyone was all right, but the driver called Jackie to let her know what had happened. With the snow and the call about the accident, Bill and Jackie were behind in their plans for the day. They decided to have dinner at Arby's—a place they never frequented. That day, Jackie had been about to bake a cake for a friend but had run out of eggs, so she wanted to pick some up while they were out. Bill asked if she wanted to just go to the Jewel near their home.

Jackie said, "No, I remember a Jewel next to that Arby's in Des Plaines. I think I was in it one time."

While Bill waited in the car, Jackie ran in for the eggs. Though she doesn't normally use the self-checkout, Bill was waiting and she needed to hurry. Standing at the self-checkout counter, she heard "Jackie? Jackie! Jackie." It was a somewhat familiar voice, but one she had not heard in a while. When she looked up, she saw Bill's aunt and uncle, Mary Ellen and George Farrell—who had moved to Michigan nearly ten years before.

Jackie went out to the car and asked Bill to come in for a minute, maintaining the surprise until he saw Mary Ellen and George for himself. Bill is used to Jackie's knowing every third person in the world, and starting conversations with everyone else, but "I can't believe it" was his reaction to this mini-reunion.

The Farrells were in the Chicago area visiting friends, staying at a hotel in Des Plaines. They were shopping for groceries at this particular Jewel because they had no car: Mary Ellen had also experienced a car spinning out of control the night before. It had landed in a ditch, and, although they were all right, the car was in the repair shop. So they went to the store nearest to their hotel. Mary Ellen and George got started much later that day than they had planned; they had slept in because of the stress of the previous day's accident. Jackie and Bill were at the store much later than they planned because of the diversity of interferences with their day. If Jackie had not been standing in a line she usually avoided, in a store where she never shopped; if Mary Ellen and George had turned another corner in the supermarket, they would not have known the others were in the very same place at the very same time. As it was, they stood next to the potato chip display and talked for two hours.

March Forth
Jen Gaber

On March 4th of 2000, I went with my friend, Kate, to see a production of *Sweeney Todd* by Strollers Theater Company in Madison, Wisconsin. I was engaged to be married that same year in September, and Kate would be in my wedding party.

I had followed Kate to Madison after visiting her many times and loving the city so much. I wanted to be one of those people bicycling along Lake Mendota and the Union Terrace. We would walk all over town for hours and see what happenings we could stumble upon:

trying on hats at an antique store on the Square, listening to live music when Jazz at Five first began, and walking up and down Broom Street looking for the Broom Street Theater, which turned out to be on Willy Street.

That night, Kate and I were stunned by the performances, especially of the actors playing Sweeney Todd and Judge Turpin. I loved the baritone singing voice of the actor playing the Judge, and felt tingly and smitten. His voice filled the room, his eyes were dark, and he had wavy hair and a prominent, masculine nose. At one point, during the curtain, he seemed to look right at me. As we left the theater, I looked over my shoulder at him standing in the lobby greeting people, and I wondered what it would be like to live a different life. My life was already taking shape, though, the reality set apart from the fantasy.

For six years, I was married to a man who loved me, but not nearly as much as he loved drinking. He had acted once, sang tenor, and read everything (having graduated with an English Literature degree). He no longer acted, didn't sing much, and never read a single book in the six years we were married.

My heart ached for him and all the living he was missing. We left the house less and less often; he never joined me for any outings. After a while he would not leave the house (outside of his job) unless he could drink where we were going. He had reached 30 beers a night and had stopped eating. Being a chef, I tried making his favorites, but they went untouched. I tried speaking with him about stopping drinking, but he would shut down completely from the conversation. Finally, I left. It felt as though he'd left me years ago. It felt as though I never completely convinced myself that this was right for me. It felt as though I had given up myself in those years.

For two years, I got my life together and enjoyed my time alone. I rebuilt a concept of who I was. I had stopped running a restaurant and being a chef to spend a year in a baking position with little responsibility. Then, when I was ready, I reclaimed a head chef position. One day, March 4th of 2008, I sat at home, sick with the flu, and bored. I had just opened a Facebook account and signed in throughout the day to entertain myself and see what my friends were doing. Each time I signed in, Facebook prompted me with "People you may know." Each time a man named Bart appeared on this list. So, sometime in the afternoon, I clicked on his photo (a picture of him with his mouth wide open as if shouting and a noose before him). I was informed that we had three friends in common. Three people, whom I had never connected to each other, except through this mysterious man about to be hanged. Curiosity killed me. I sent him a message to ask about how he knew my friends. I heard back instantly! He had been in *Richard III* with Matthew, *Assassins* with Amber, and *Sweeney Todd* with Bob. We chatted back and forth all day and set a time to meet for coffee.

After that day, I discovered a recorded copy of *Sweeney Todd* on his video shelf. We watched it, and there he was, the same Judge Turpin that had caught my eye and my wonder eight years before!

Bart and I have been together for two years now. I am so grateful for this man who sings with me in choir, who acts in two or three productions a year, reads two books a week, always joins me on outings, and lives life with me. I found out what it would be like to live that different life, and it is wonderful!

Sequoya Library
Jean Martinelli

About 30 years ago, I became friends with Barb Nichols, a colleague in the English department at West High School. I certainly didn't know at that time that we would both go through hard times in each of our marriages, followed by both divorces and dating problems. Anyway, we became soul mates. When Barb met and married someone within six months of their meeting, I was in a very bad place. Somehow, our paths diverged, especially when she started law school.

After Barb was diagnosed with ovarian cancer, she and I became close again and routinely went out to dinner or lunch, together with another close friend, Sally. Unfortunately, about ten years ago, after a five year battle with the cancer, Barb Nichols died.

About a week after Barb died, when I was alone in the laundry room, I felt someone put an arm around my waist. Thinking it was my husband trying to startle me, I quickly turned around to scold him. Nobody was there. I was left to wonder whether Barb was reaching out to me.

Last year, volunteering for Sequoya Library's book sale, I was shelving books with a group of eight women. As I sat there, putting stickers on a stack of books, I heard a worker say, "Oh what a shame! Someone's left some wedding pictures in this book."

I sardonically said, "Oh, don't throw them away. Someone here may know the bride."

In an equally cynical fashion, my cohort thrust the pictures at me and said, "Here."

With shock, I saw that the photos were of my dear friend Barb and her husband Donald Nichols on their wedding day. Looking at these pictures, which I had never seen before, I felt goose bumps spreading all over my limbs. For almost an hour I could hardly speak. As soon as I arrived home, I called Sally and told her the story. She was equally astounded and pleased to learn that there were enough photos for each of us.

I was left to wonder whether this was just coincidence or whether once again my soul mate was at work.

Calico Comforters
Kate Gould

While I was growing up, we always had a cat in the family. When my mom died, during the week before her funeral, my dad and I were both visited by calico cats. His surprise visitor appeared outside the bathroom door on the second floor of his house, the morning after Mom died. Dad thought he had probably left a door open, but he was startled nonetheless. That same cat rested on a little stone fence outside his kitchen window, every morning until Mom's funeral.

Meanwhile, 60 miles away, I coped with my mom's death by working in my garden. The first day, a stray calico cat kept me company while I worked, and she also showed up each day until the funeral. I named her Irene, in my mom's memory. Although Dad and I subsequently learned that each of our visitors belonged to neighbors, we loved their timely visits.

Six months later, we held Thanksgiving dinner at my house. We were missing Mom, who had always hosted Thanksgiving, and she was very much in our thoughts and conversations. During the meal we heard a "meow." On the deck outside the dining room was Irene the cat! I hadn't seen her since Mom's funeral. Not only was I surprised to see her, but she had to scale a six-foot fence to get into the enclosed deck. My daughter let her in, and Irene made her way around the table, rubbing against everyone. We were pleased to see her, and my daughter said, "Well, Grandma's here after all!" We like to think she was.

Navid and Ian
Bobbi Zehner

Elspeth, originally from England, agreed to accompany Bobbi on a Cystic Fibrosis 5K walk one lovely spring day. Each year Bobbi walks with Mohila, another friend, whom Elspeth had met briefly a few other times. This particular year Mohila's friend Zari was also on the walk. As the four of them ambled along, Zari mentioned her son Navid, Elspeth gasped, "You're Navid's mother?"

Elspeth knew Navid exceptionally well. He had been her son Ian's closest friend since childhood, but Elspeth had never met Zari--even though the boys had been roommates at one time. The two women had much to talk about.

An interesting twist was that as these two women walked and talked, their sons were vacationing together in England, staying with Elspeth's family. As soon as she got home, Elspeth phoned Ian and Navid in England to tell them about meeting Zari on the Cystic Fibrosis Walk: a delightful stroll for a worthy cause.

The Sherpa and the Polar Bear
Brad Barham

During the summer of 1977, a recent college graduate, I was traveling in Peru. I planned to go backpacking in the Callejon de Huaylas, known as the Peruvian Switzerland. The peaks of the highest mountains in this range are from 23,000 to 25,000 feet. I was going to hike from the base of one of the peaks up above the glacier line to about 18,000 feet.

That first day in, I was taking a truck ride up to the base camp where I was going to start my climb. Hopping into the back of a truck, I came face-to-face with the sherpa for a German mountain climbing team. Waskar was returning to the Germans' base camp with supplies: kerosene in a ten gallon container, a large box, and a heavy backpack crammed with who knows what. We were heading up into the mountains, about a ten-mile drive up the road. After about five miles, we reached an army checkpoint. There they told us we had to turn around and go back, because crews were doing road work that day.

At this news, Waskar looked very forlorn. Besides five more miles to go, he had 3,000 feet still to climb--with the ten-gallon container of kerosene, the large box, and the heavy backpack. I said, "I'll help you." We strapped the box around him with a rope. Balancing his backpack on top of my backpack, so it was above my head, we secured it with a bungee cord. We found a very strong stick to put through the handle of the kerosene container and carried it up the mountain in tandem. We traded sides every 500 yards or so, because carrying a ten-gallon container on a stick between two people is a lot of work, when trying to keep your footwork on rough terrain.

But I was 21--maybe not strapping, but strong--and we made it to the top of the trail where I was going to spend the night. We were at the first of two lakes--the Llanganuco lakes--and so we stashed the kerosene and the box there. With only the backpack now, we hiked the rest of the way to the base camp to meet up with the German team and the other five sherpas.

Waskar told the head sherpa how I had helped, where we stashed the gear, and they were all grateful. The sherpas then invited me into the main tent, where they were preparing food and getting ready for the next day's hike. They planned to make another base camp, and then climb a 22,000 foot peak. They invited me to spend the night in their tent. They were drinking. I didn't drink, because at 13,000 feet I was finding it hard enough to get oxygen. They spoke Spanish and Quechua whenever they didn't want me to understand, which meant half the time I was in the dark. In Spanish, they bombarded me with questions about whether they could get jobs in the United States. Could I help them? How would one get across the border? All numbers were in Spanish, so I always knew when they were talking economics. We had a nice time talking late into the night.

The next morning, they packed up much of their gear and headed up to their next base camp. I left my backpack at the campsite and hiked up to the glacier line, where there were beautiful turquoise lakes and fantastic mountain scenery. I could see many snowcapped peaks. I climbed as high as 18,000 feet. When I climbed back down to the campsite, it was about 4:30 in the afternoon. As I picked up my backpack, I was surprised by a guy in a uniform. Marching up to me, he said in Spanish, "I'm a park ranger."

I answered in Spanish, "You're kidding. There are no park rangers in Peru."

And, he said, "I am a park ranger."

"Okay, what do you want?" I asked.

He said, "It's illegal to camp on this side of the stream."

The stream that ran down into this little valley was fifty or sixty feet wide, no deeper than your knees at any point.

The ranger repeated, "It's illegal to camp on this side. You cannot have any of this gear here--it's all illegal. I will come back with a truck and confiscate it, if it is not moved to the other side."

I thought, "Oh, crap--what am I going to do with all this stuff!"

The Germans had left fifteen containers, and the closest bridge to cross the stream was a mile down. Doing the math, I figured that even if I took two things at once, I would be walking twenty or thirty miles to move everything down to the bridge crossing. It wasn't going to work. I packed everything up as compactly as I could and carried it to the edge of the stream. I took a breath, put my foot into the stream, and screamed as loudly as I could! The water was frigid--thirty-four degrees maybe--and I thought,"Ugh, what am I going to do?"

All of a sudden I heard, "¿Qué pasa?"

I looked up and there was this weathered older man, with a gray beard and a backpack, saying "¿Qué pasa?"

And I said, "¿Habla ingles?"

"Yeah, I'm from Iceland. Whatcha' doin'?"

And I said, "Just trying to figure out how I'm going to get all this stuff across a freezing stream."

He said, "No problem. I'm a polar bear."

I said, "That's cool," thinking, And I'm Mickey Mouse.

He must have read my mind, because he asserted, "No, no, I am a polar bear!"

"So what's a polar bear?" I asked.

"A polar bear is somebody who jumps into the glacial waters when they melt every winter in Iceland. I do it every year. I'll have no problem taking this stuff across."

Oh, there is a God, and he is from Iceland, and he has a haggard face, and he has a beard.

The polar bear picked up the first load and said, "I might as well go all the way across. Then you carry halfway to me and go back for more. That way, you're not fording the whole stream."

I took two steps into the stream and screamed again as loudly as I could. Polar Bear came all the way across, took that box from me, and carried it to the other side. The end result was that he carried fifteen boxes nine-tenths of the way across the stream. I would jump back onto land and hold my feet. The longest I was ever in the water was five seconds, while he was in the icy stream for a full minute with each crossing.

When he finished, about half an hour later, he said, "Okay, I'm going to go now." He headed on down the valley, while I camped out during the night. I'm pretty sure that that was one of the more remarkable experiences of my life--when I might have met God on a sojourn, and he was a polar bear from Iceland.

Chapter Two

There is no such thing as chance; and what seems to us merest accident springs from the deepest source of destiny.

Frederick Schiller (1759-1805)

Clear Across the Country
Shoshauna Shy

I was living in a communal household in Wisconsin with a couple, Ben and Irene. Our friend Gil was expected to arrive from the East Coast, for a short stay with us, on his way to a new teaching job in Illinois. His wife, Eva, also our friend, was planning to join him later. However, not long after Gil landed on our doorstep, he received a call from Eva telling him that she wanted out of their marriage, and she would not be following him to Illinois. What had transpired between them that led to this drastic decision was a mystery to Ben, Irene and me - -and apparently a great shock to Gil.

He tried to contact her by phone, but she wouldn't take his calls. Eventually, Gil had to leave our house to meet his new obligations in Illinois. Meanwhile, Ben and Irene also tried to reach Eva to find out what happened and what she was going to do next. She didn't return their phone calls, either.

Several weeks later, Ben and Irene set out on a road trip to the West Coast, still mystified and disheartened by this strange turn of events in their friends' lives. After nearly a week of traveling, they arrived in California. Driving through Big Sur, they elected to stay the night in one of the many campgrounds along the coastline. While they were setting up their tent, a car pulled into the campsite next to them, and they heard a very familiar female voice. There was Eva--and a new man--pitching a tent. Surprised but relieved to see her, Ben and Irene spent the entire night with Eva and her lover around a campfire, catching up on the summer's events, and trying to come to terms with how this fracture in friendship had affected all of them.

Karl Rausch's Restaurant
Bobbi Zehner

Shortly after Larry and I moved to Madison, Wisconsin, Elaine called from Chicago, inviting us to meet Dennis and her at the Milwaukee

Zoo. Elaine and I had worked together for many years before she left the company. I was eager to see her again; I had missed her quick wit and loving spirit.

So, after a pleasant summer's day spent at the surprisingly empty zoo grounds, we decided to extend our camaraderie by dining together. But because not one of the four of us had ever been to Milwaukee, we didn't know where to eat. Pulling up to a stop light, Dennis called out the car window to a pedestrian, "Can you suggest a good restaurant around here?"

"Karl Rausch's," the friendly man answered as he crossed the street. "Go two blocks and hang a right." We chuckled among ourselves, wondering if his last name might not just be Rausch!

Rausch's window posted an appealing menu. Our stomachs were growling. Being under-dressed, in zoo attire, didn't faze us one bit. It was a large restaurant, and we were early. When we were seated on the second floor, away from the high volume of arriving diners, it occurred to us that our casual attire might not have been seen as good for business. Whether the helpful pedestrian was related to the restaurant's owner or not, his tip was providential. The food and service were superb.

While Elaine was bringing me up-to-date on the work world I had left in Chicago, I asked how our mutual friend Kathy Meehan was doing. Elaine said, "I invited Kathy to come to the zoo with us today, knowing she'd like to see you, too, but she had some kind of a family dealie-do to attend."

"Oh, I would love to see her," I gushed.

In a startled voice, with eyes wide open, Elaine sputtered, "Well, as a matter of fact, you can, because there she is!"

Being seated at a table directly across from us were Kathy Meehan and a group of women, most of whom had driven from Chicago to attend a bridal shower on the second floor of Karl Rausch's--in Milwaukee!

An old Swedish proverb says, "The afternoon knows what the morning never suspected." In this case, however, it was the evening that delivered a welcome surprise!

Reunion on the Interstate
Sparrow Senty

Al and I were on the Interstate in Ohio, driving back to Wisconsin from Connecticut, after attending the funeral services of my niece who had died unexpectedly. The weather forecast was ominous: October rains with freezing temperatures. So Al and I decided to head farther south to Highway 80, rather than to stay north closer to the lakes and risk icy roads.

Now picture this: we're breezing along a little after lunch time, when this station wagon passes us, going all out down the road--zoom zoom. Al thought the station wagon looked kind of familiar. As it was getting farther and farther away, he wondered aloud, "Can that be my brother Roger?" Roger lives in Iowa.

"What would he be doing out here?"

Curious, Al speeds up and as we get closer, we see a "Brown for ssembly" bumper sticker. Brown is the name of Roger's son-in-law, who had run for the Iowa State Assembly.

"It is my brother!" Al says.

We speed up even more, but Roger doesn't recognize us, so we pull alongside on his right. We toot our horn and wave. It takes Roger and his wife a minute to realize that it's us. Laughing, we then lead them off the highway at the next exit, where we have a cup of coffee together, and a short visit.

They were on their way back home to Iowa from Maine. Neither of us had known that we would be on the East Coast at the same time. Had it not been for weather conditions, and the sad circumstances that took us out east, Al and I would never have been on that highway. Had Roger and his wife not been looking for property in Maine, this is one family reunion that would never have happened.

Have We Met Somewhere Before?
Pat Meyer

As I entered T. J. Maxx's, I used the clips on my new Italian leather handbag to secure it to the basket of the store's shopping cart. For added protection, I covered the bag with my heavy black overcoat, never leaving the cart's side for a moment. I bent down once to look at an item from a lower shelf, and, in that instant, a young woman who must have been following me reached under the coat, unclipped the bag, and bolted her way through the store. I popped up and ran after her, yelling, "Stop her! Stop her! She stole my purse!"

From among the many customers, two women emerged simultaneously to corner the thief. Surrounded by the three of us, the miscreant surrendered the handbag by shoving it at me. We managed to detain her until the store security arrived. Realizing that we actually were powerless, the culprit made a hasty retreat while hurling vile epithets over her shoulder.

With our adrenaline still pumping, we three turned to introduce ourselves to each other. The first woman, like me, was a retired high school English teacher and looked familiar. We quickly figured out that we shared a close friend in common and had met previously. Oddly enough, the second woman also looked vaguely familiar, and I said, "I have the feeling we've met somewhere before, too."

To which she replied with a impish grin, "Yes, we have. I work at the hospital and I prepped you for your colonoscopy."

Let's hope I remembered to say thank you.

Ships in the Night
Robert Wood

Background: A night spent in conversation until dawn with a mentor, my seventh grade teacher, on her death bed, in which she convinced me to consider being a teacher. Inspired by her, I enrolled in a graduate program that led to an intern teaching position in Huddersfield, England the following year. The initial placement was a fifth grade classroom, but it did not provide the setting for learning the open-classroom model, which had attracted me to that school.

I was able to switch to a first grade setting in another school, which coincidentally was the school in which another American had been placed through the same program to provide the open-class-room experience. This teacher had been called in at the last minute and asked to switch semesters. The original intern had met an untimely death. Pat was more highly skilled to teach at this level than I, and she had the good heart to help me adjust. She also emanated an astounding beauty, like a precious flower I had traveled the world over to find.

The year was 1973, the two innocents both had partners back in the United States. However, the torch had been lit. While it may have flickered now and again over the years, it has never been extinguished. To this day, Pat and I--those two young interns--are still happily married.

A small change of circumstances here or there and our ships would no doubt have passed in the night.

Cisternino
Bobbi Zehner

Twelve of us from across the U.S. met in Cisternino, Italy, where we were volunteering to help teenagers practice their English speaking skills. We had been together for almost a week, sharing a daily 35-minute van ride to and from the high school. One morning, Gina, from New York City, was in a particularly feisty mood and I teased, "You must have been a handful for the teachers yourself when you were a kid!"

"No way," said Gina. "The nuns at Sacred Heart wouldn't let me do a thing. They were really tough."

"Sacred Heart in New Jersey?" piped up Carol. The answer to that question brought with it the revelation that Carol's Aunt May, in New Jersey, had been Gina's mother's very best lifelong friend, until Aunt May's death 15 years earlier. I witnessed, and shared, the thrill of discovery as Gina and Carol compared overlapping memories. They had attended the same family events, like weddings and funerals, and knew many of the same people, without ever having been introduced. And here they were riding in a van, heading to a small town in southern Italy to do volunteer work together. It became obvious that the two women were planning to get together back east when our trip was over.

A few days later, spunky Gina showed up for our evening meal with a fresh ricotta cheese cake. The hotel had a set menu, including dessert, so we were at a loss as to how to share it. Winking at me, Gina cornered a waiter and told him it was my birthday. "Bene, bene," he said. Then he sliced and served the cheese cake, while my colleagues croaked out a pitiful rendition of "Happy Birthday."

We had been sharing the hotel dining room for almost a week with a contingent of about 30 Germans. We didn't speak their language and they didn't seem interested in speaking ours, so we nodded our greetings and smiled pleasantly in passing. When they saw that it was my birthday, the German contingent suddenly went into action, dragging me from my seat to stand between two of their members, whose birthdays actually were that day. In German, they sang "Happy Birthday" in three part harmony. They were a traveling choir. They had the waiter pour champagne for everyone. A shared birthday and a little bubbly had warmed us all.

One enthusiastic singer approached, asking if anyone in our group was from California--Los Altos, California. "Oddly enough, yes." I smiled and pointed her in Marianne's direction.

Once I was back home in the States, Marianne sent the following e-mail:

"Do you remember the German lady from your birthday party (wink, wink) who chatted with me because she had connections in Los Altos? I had her write down their names for the proverbial just in case...Well, wouldn't you know that when I took a closer look at the name, I thought it sounded vaguely familiar. Turns out it's the house right behind mine, and the woman is an extended family member of the neighbors I speak to once every half century or so. Around Oktoberfest they get a little lively and the singing continues well into the evening. I'm sorry I didn't make the connection on the spot for the dear woman. I guess my brain was on pasta-carb overload."

I later also got an e-mail from Carol, saying that her 53 year old cousin had suddenly died. Terribly sad though it was, she got to see Gina at the memorial service. They spent most of the luncheon together talking. Gina's mother and brother were present and knew almost everyone there, including Carol.

Opportunity Not Missed
Vivian Fenner-Evans

I have traveled extensively in Central and South America. In 1981, I was living in Brazil with my Brazilian husband, whom I had met while traveling. One day on a street corner in Salvador, Bahia, I saw a tall, blonde woman with hair down to her waist, shining like a lighthouse. In those days, there were very few blondes in Bahia, so I approached her to find out who she was and why she was there. Her name was Ann, and she was teaching English at ACEBEU (Associacao Cultural Brazil Estados Unidos). I told her that, in 1974, I had traveled with a journalist named Jack Epstein, who wrote one of the first budget travel guides to Latin America, called *Along the Gringo Trail*. Jack also had taught English at ACEBEU.

Ann said excitedly, "Jack Epstein is in town. I just met him." He was traveling with another journalist and was getting ready to leave. I asked Ann to have Jack contact me. He was happy to learn that I was in town and said that he would meet for drinks on the beach that night. He would be alone, though, because his writing partner, Jim Evans, had gone to a nearby island.

That evening, Jack told us about all that he and Jim had done, including being investigated for wearing the wrong clothing to the second presidential inauguration of Gen. Augusto Pinochet, the former Chilean dictator.

By 1985, I had divorced the Brazilian and relocated to San Francisco. A friend whom I had met in Brazil asked to have his 40th birthday party at my house. One of his friends was Jim Evans, the journalist whom I almost had met nearly four years earlier. As it turned out, Jim lived two blocks from my flat. We marveled at meeting in San Francisco after having come close to meeting in Brazil. As we discovered our many common interests, we began dating. Jim and I just celebrated our 23rd wedding anniversary.

Lake County, Illinois
Sheryl Mares

Jim took me on a whirlwind romantic trip to Italy to celebrate our 25th wedding anniversary. It was our first big trip, sans children, in all those years.

We flew to Rome and devoured every second of our time there. From Rome we took a train to Venice and loved that magical city, too. I still can't believe that people live there and enjoy that beauty every day of their lives. Our last stop, which turned out to be our favorite, was Florence.

Jim and I boarded a train early in the morning. Our seats faced each other with a table between us. We got comfortable--took out our snacks and books and waited for the train to leave the station. Across the aisle and one row back was another American couple, with the last two empty seats in the car next to them.

Another couple boarded at the very last minute. Though I had my nose in my book, I heard a very recognizable, annoying, Fran Dresher-ish voice that I immediately recognized from our past. Let's call her Margaret and her husband Steve.

As newlyweds, we had bought a townhouse with a Deerfield mailing address in unincorporated Lake County, Illinois. It always sounded better to tell people you lived in Deerfield rather than unincorporated Lake County, so that's what we all did. Steve and Margaret were our neighbors there.

As Steve and Margaret took their seats, the American couple sharing their area asked where they were from. Margaret said "Deerfield."

Jim turned around and said, "No, you aren't. You live in unincorporated Lake County!"

We spent the last three nights of our trip dining with them and the other American couple. By the end of the trip, I didn't even notice how annoying Margaret's voice was!

Chapter Three

A small change of circumstances here or there and
our ships would no doubt have passed in the night.

Robert Wood

What's Up, Johnny Mack?
Linda Butler

In 1973, Vinni Daniels was a high school band director in Rochester, New York. Born and raised in Louisiana, where nicknames were popular, for his first ten years of teaching, Vinni often used Johnny Mack, as a generic name for many of his students. "What's up, Johnny Mack?"

And a kid would respond, "Nothing's going on, Johnny Moe."

In 1981, Vinni transferred to a different high school, where he worked until 2003. That year, Vinni happened to be in a grocery store, when a tall husky fellow came up behind him and whispered, "What's up, Johnny Mack?"

Vinni replied, "Nothing's going on, Johnny Moe."

"Johnny Moe" was Vinni's 40-something-year-old former student from Rochester, New York, who affectionately recognized his old high school band teacher.

Saved by the Beach
Shoshauna Shy

On a family road trip from Wisconsin to Cape Cod, our 13-year-old daughter Mikaela was cracking jokes that only a 13-year-old girl would think funny. Her 15-year-old brother was rolling his eyes. Finally I said, "You know, you could really use somebody your own age here, my dear," as we pulled into a parking lot at a beach.

We climbed out of the mini-van, and heard a voice yell, "Hello, you guys!" There stood one of our neighbors. She announced that her entire family was down by the shore, including her 13-year-old daughter with whom Mikaela bused to middle school every day.

Our two families spent an enjoyable afternoon and evening meal together. Now if only I could win the lottery the same way!

Angie's Story
Gail Juszczak

I met Mike when I was 27 years old. We had both been married previously for short periods of time. He had a daughter from his first marriage but had given up custody for several reasons. His ex-wife's new husband wanted to adopt the daughter, Angie. Mike had tried to keep in contact with Angie for several years without success. His letters and gifts were always returned by his ex-wife.

Mike and I married when I was 30 years old. I had not had children, but really wanted them. We tried to get pregnant, but we did not have success. I had known about Mike's daughter and was somewhat jealous, although I realized it was not logical. However, I still was.

While Mike and I were living in Cottage Grove, we decided to go to Lake Mills to swim on a beautiful Saturday in June. At Sandy Beach, we lay on the white sand for a while. Then I decided to go out into the lake, but Mike stayed on the blanket. As I walked out, a young lady with a small flotation raft was taunting a friend staying closer to shore. I turned to the friend, in comfort, and began a conversation with her.

I let her know that I was an art teacher. She told me that she liked art and even explained about a weaving that she had created. She was in 8th grade and scared about going to high school. I talked to her about how changes are hard, but that I knew she would do fine. She asked if I had children. I said that we were trying, but were not able to yet.

She said, "Don't have a boy! I have a new brother and he is a pain."

We talked for 30 minutes. This has not ever happened, before or since, that I talked so long and intimately with someone I had just met. At the end of the conversation, she introduced herself, saying her name was Angie.

"Why, I know of a girl named Angie. Angie, what is your last name?" Her last name sounded very familiar.

Mike, my husband, was soaking in the sun while Angie and I talked. Returning to the blanket, I asked him what his daughter's last name was. The miracle was that I had been talking to my husband's daughter for half an hour, without knowing it.

I told him he needed to go say something to her. He said no. "She has one dad and that is enough. Besides, what can I say?"

So I went back into the water and asked Angie if her mom's name happened to be Sue. She said, "Yes. Why, do you know my Mom?"

I said, "No, but my husband does. Do you know the name Mike Juszczak?"

She said no, and I left it at that. When she left the beach, she waved and yelled good-bye.

Twenty years later, I still am shocked by this miracle. And happy. After this day at Sandy Beach, Angie approached her mother, asking her about Mike. She then wrote a letter to Mike's parents and has stayed in contact with them ever since. Through them, we have Angie's photo hanging proudly in our home. Over the years, we have seen Angie's graduation picture, her wedding pictures, and now the new baby pictures. I do feel blessed.

Meanwhile, Mike and I have adopted a child of our own: a beautiful, talented and challenging daughter. But we still hope to one day meet Angie again.

The Tale of Sir Allard
Carolyn Zahn-Waxler

Carolyn Zahn-Waxler shares the story of her great-grandfather, Alex Johnson, and the legacy of a "fine trotter" named Sir Allard.

My great-grandfather, Alex Johnson, married my great-grandmother, Julia Anderson, in 1895. The Anderson family was prominent in the village of Ephraim in Door County, Wisconsin. Conscious of their status in the community, they may have fussed a bit when Julia married Alex and moved to Sturgeon Bay, 30 miles to the south. He was a Swede and a blacksmith, which would have placed him a rung or two beneath the Andersons on the social ladder. However, Alex had a certain distinction that put him in a class of his own. Alex, who enjoyed horse racing, owned a fine trotter named Sir Allard— Sturgeon Bay's fastest trotting horse, according to Sir Allard's newspaper obituary.

Sir Allard died suddenly at the age of seven from an intestinal blockage caused by limestone deposits. When the post-mortem was performed, two stones weighing three-quarters of a pound each were found in his lower stomach. How they came to reside there was a mystery.

Alex Johnson's beloved horse was buried near the stable in the backyard of the Johnson homestead. Sir Allard was mourned as a family member. Throughout that day, the people of Sturgeon Bay stopped by to pay their respects. His death warranted two articles in the *Door County Advocate*. Sir Allard was by all accounts a noble steed and a loss to the community.

Carolyn brings Sir Allard's story and legacy forward 100 years. Carolyn and her sister Barbara had grown up in a house one block away from her great-grandparents and were familiar with the stories about Sir Allard. As a child, Barbara and a playmate, who lived in the Johnson house at the time, searched without success for the horse's bones. Carolyn and Barbara remained close to their cousins Emily and Kay. A phone call from Emily began the process of connecting Sir Allard to several new generations: both family and strangers.

One day my cousin Emily called, breathless with excitement. Her good friend Joan had heard from someone that Jack, a young boy who had lived in the old Johnson house some years earlier, had had a dream about a horse buried under the garage in his backyard. We cannot know for certain if Jack had also heard stories about the horse from others nearby, for it may have still been part of the neighborhood lore. In any event, Sir Allard had infiltrated Jack's dream world.

Emily's story did not end there. She told me about Dr. Todd, the new dermatologist in town, who was a recent Madison transplant. Dr. Todd had rented space in the Johnson house earlier when she was trying to decide about opening a practice in Sturgeon Bay. She must have heard the story about Jack's dream from the homeowners at the time and relayed it to one of her patients. That patient was Emily's son Eddy. Eddy asked the dermatologist the location of the house; it was one he knew well--the Johnson homestead. Eddy told Dr. Todd that the house had belonged to his great-great-grandfather, and that indeed there was a horse buried there.

Several weeks later, my husband Morris and I were at a dinner party at a home in Sturgeon Bay. George, the host, was a man whom Morris had met in the locker room of the local fitness center. George is an administrative judge in Madison, and his wife, Cecelia, is a musician.

Cecelia's sister Alice was also there, with her husband and children. They had traveled from Germany to visit her mother-in-law, Hannah, who had recently moved to Sturgeon Bay. Other friends, some with Madison roots, were also at the party.

I was chatting with Hannah about Sturgeon Bay and how great my neighborhood was when I was a child. I mentioned the location of our old home—the corner of South 8th Avenue and Oregon Street. "Oh," she said, "I live at the corner of 9th and Oregon!" Hannah was living in Grandpa Johnson's old house. She then told me the same story I had heard from Emily, about Jack's dream of a buried horse—and I told her about Sir Allard. She was stunned.

At that point, another guest arrived—the dermatologist, Dr. Todd. She heard us talking about the house and the horse and joined the discussion, adding her own piece: that she had also lived in that house. This was the first time that Hannah and Dr. Todd had met.

After dinner, some of the guests strolled down the beach to watch the fireworks, passing the house of Emily's friend Joan, who initially had told Emily about Jack's dream.

None of these people had known each other before. They came together at a dinner party simply because Morris and George had met in a locker room. It is hard to believe that the tale of Sir Allard is well-known in contemporary Sturgeon Bay. But he has certainly captured the imagination of a diverse, unrelated group of people. It's gratifying to know that Sir Allard still lives on in the minds of others.

Haagen-Dazs Ice Cream Shop
Kate Conklin Corcoran

Ruth Robarts, a law school dean, was visiting her daughter Kate, who lives in Japan. Each year, when Ruth visits, the two of them take a side trip to somewhere warm. In 2008, Thailand was their destination of choice. On their sight-seeing tour in Bangkok, they found themselves at a temple with thousands of other people from all over the world. Within the grounds of the temple—for some global enterprise reason—was a Haagen-Dazs ice cream shop.

While Ruth and Kate felt a little embarrassed, they did stand in line for ice cream. Over the noise of the crowd, Ruth heard someone calling her name. The only person Ruth knew in Thailand was her daughter Kate, right beside her. And then she heard her name again and turned to see Notesong, a recent law school grad from Wisconsin. Notesong, with her husband and all of her Thai relatives were visiting the temple, and the Haagen-Dazs shop, on the same day.

Happenstance in Amsterdam
Sherry Brenner

Four years after my divorce, I made my maiden voyage to Europe.

My marriage had been an abusive one, but in the 1950s this subject was not yet publicly acknowledged. By 1970 divorce was still frowned upon, but the marriage had ended, burned out. My self-confidence was at low ebb.

By 1976, I'd begun to gather strength and try out my wings. I discovered a curiosity in myself and soon was inspired to explore Europe. My initial trip to Europe was my "coming out." I traveled through seven countries in five weeks, using the Eurail pass and staying in bed and breakfast establishments. It was everything I had hoped for--and more. I found I could problem-solve; I could make new friends; I could count on myself.

One evening, I was dining in a restaurant in Amsterdam, a quaint old place on a side street. Sitting at my table alone, in one of the tiny rooms, I contentedly pulled out my postcards and started writing to some friends. As a woman traveling alone, I found reading a book or writing to be pleasant dinner company. Having something to do at a restaurant table made me feel less awkward. That night, sitting across from me, was a couple, obviously in love and conversing animatedly. For a minute, I felt a lonely longing, and then I went back to my writing.

Two years later, I met Mel. He was very interested in my tales about European travel, so much so that we decided to take a trip there together. Now I was back in Amsterdam, this time with Mel. We were joyously in love, and I was thrilled at being able to share this experience with him. As we were walking the streets of Amsterdam one night, looking for a place to eat, I noticed a restaurant that looked familiar and suggested we eat there. When the host greeted us at the door, my heart gave a flip of recognition.

We were directed into a small room, and I thought to myself, "Can this really be happening?"

I said to Mel, "This is the same room I was in two years ago." This time I was seated at the exact table I had sat at two years ago: now with the man I loved. I looked across to where I'd last seen that other loving couple. There sat a single woman, wrapping her alone-ness cozily around her as she wrote postcards to her friends

Similar Tastes
Franki Black

We not only shared the same name but, years before we met, we shared the same boyfriend. Many years after that, we learnt that we had another very odd thing in common. Such is the nature of my friendship with Franci. It was something that must have been etched in the stars because when we finally met, we knew that we shared something special.

I was 14 years old and on holiday with my longtime friend, Jacky. We stayed with her family in a popular seaside village called Kenton-on-Sea. During summer, this sleepy town pulsated to life as huge marquee tents emerged all along the beach: all in the name of teenage indulgences. Glorious! At one of these marquee parties, I spotted a short, sun-kissed, blue-eyed boy named Kyle. His stripy rugby jersey and high-pitched voice were enough to bowl me over and, before I knew it, I was in the middle of a short-lived holiday romance. Kyle was the first person to say her name: Franci. She was his high school girlfriend, who happened to come from the most exotic place on earth, Zambia. How could I even compare?

After our whirlwind vacation, Jacky and I returned to the reality of school. Through the grapevine I learnt that Franci, inevitably, had heard about me--for better or for worse.

Years later, I graduated from high school and moved into Serruria, a university hostel, for the beginning of a four-year degree in Politics. To my utter surprise, there she was: Franci. We introduced ourselves. I was certain she would hate me, but instead she radiated a look that said, "I am so happy to meet you." Through the awkward rituals of student initiation, we observed each other from a distance. Slowly but surely, we drew closer to one another. It was the beginning of a wonderful friendship.

As happens in the exciting, romance-tinted air of campus life, Franci fell deeply in love with the stocky and charming Graeme. And I met my long-term, Greek-blooded boyfriend, Niko. As freshman oblivion turned into third-year reality checks, Franci and Graeme's passionate relationship started to falter. At the same time, I was dealing with my wandering boyfriend.

By the time our romances came to an end, Franci and I were studying in different towns. But when I needed a friend to cry to during the early hours of the morning, Franci was always there with a comforting word. We indulged in everything from spontaneous road trips to lavish wine tours to deep, meaningful conversations. One of these conversations led to a bizarre revelation, which brings me to the final coincidence of our friendship.

When I was five years old, my parents sent me to Rhenish Pre-Primary School to improve my hold on the English language. As English was my second language, I was a nervous wreck, so I instantly picked the one non-English speaking girl as my best friend. Her name was Boram Kim, and she was a master pianist, a prodigy from South Korea. Boram and I were inseparable. She would accompany me on family vacations, and I would spend many afternoons playing at her house.

One day Boram's family invited my sister, Marguerite, and me to a Sunday lunch. Boram's extended South Korean family was seated at the table. Marguerite and I felt incredibly honored to be a part of this occasion. That was, until the traditional fish dish arrived. It was so inedible to our western palates that both Marguerite and I subtly transferred the fish from our mouths to our napkins. Nonchalantly, we excused ourselves from the table and met in the bathroom in a panicked state. Somehow we pulled off an exit strategy and eluded the dreaded fish dish.

Sadly, I left town after my one year of friendship with Boram, because my dad was transferred to another university. I never saw her again. Boram's family eventually returned to South Korea, where her musical talent landed her a scholarship at an American university.

Years later, Franci and I were having the "childhood" talk. She mentioned that her parents sent her to Rhenish Primary School when they still lived in South Africa. Franci entered Rhenish Primary School exactly one year after me, another nervous wreck. To her delight, she spotted a lonely South Korean girl. Her name was Boram Kim -- and Franci became Boram's new best friend.

To this day, Franci and I still laugh about all the strange coincidences that have shaped our friendship. We laugh about the butterflies we shared for a certain boy named Kyle, and we laugh about the coincidence of having had a shared childhood friend. But mostly, we laugh about the dreaded fish dish that Franci had the pleasure of tasting--a year after me.

Chapter Four

Is there something about the way we form personal connections that heightens the likelihood of such synchronicities?

Carolyn Zahn-Waxler

Seaside
Nancy Hertel

One summer, my daughter Kerry and her husband Doug, who live in Corvallis, Oregon, arranged for our whole family to vacation together. We rented a house near Seaside, Oregon, a tiny town with a gorgeous view of the ocean. When we went into Seaside to walk the beach, my mother-in-law Dorothy decided to wait in a restaurant until we all came back from our stroll. While she was sitting in the restaurant, a couple approached her and said, "Hi, Dorothy." Surprised at hearing her name, Dorothy turned to see the smile of friends from Waverly, Iowa: our home town.

Returning from our walk, we were surprised to see Judge Riffle and his wife chatting with Dorothy. Semi-retired, they lived part-time in Portland, in order to be closer to family. That day, they, too, had decided to go to over to the coast specifically to visit Seaside, a sweet little town to stop for lunch or a stroll along the beach.

Portaging the Boundary Waters
Marilee Sushoreba

I met Bruce when I was in college. Of Finnish descent, he had all of the telltale features: big blue eyes, blonde hair, broad shoulders, an arresting smile, and an easy laugh. An ace outdoorsman, he had honed the skills characteristic of someone comfortable in nature through years of working as a counselor at a camp for kids.

After graduation, Bruce and I ended up working together at a home for youth temporarily living away from their families. It was there that I came to know his legendary outdoor skills first-hand. One of our first assignments was to take a small group of residents for a long weekend of canoeing and camping into the Boundary Waters Canoe Area, a rugged wilderness area in northeastern Minnesota consisting of a vast web of over 1200 lakes connected by trails. More than once, Bruce's prowess was pressed into service on the trip as we paddled the many miles of rough lakes, rivers, and marshes, established camps in craggy areas, and built fires to feed our intrepid group and to stay warm.

But it was Bruce's ability to portage the rocky miles between lakes that amazed me the most. Under normal circumstances, most people would shudder at the thought of hauling 30-40 pounds of gear on their backs while simultaneously carrying a canoe on their shoulders. It is hard work, made harder still by twists and turns of narrow paths, the unrelenting up and down of hills, and the challenge of negotiating large exposed rocks and roots along the trails.

Bruce, however, made portaging look like child's sport, traversing the rugged terrain with ease and great speed. Astonishingly, he also did this without the assistance of his hands. He would simply cross his arms in front of his chest to create a solid foundation for the canoe to rest on and take off, never once reaching for the gunnels to help maintain the boat's balance to prevent it from falling. Gradually, we grew accustomed to the image of Bruce crashing through the woods with crossed arms, canoe on top, coming up the other end of the portage looking easy with a smile on his face, but it never ceased to amuse us.

We worked together for another year or two after that trip until the Peace Corps called Bruce to Nepal for a number of years and an adventure drew me to South America. We stayed in touch at first, but the miles and demanding experiences eventually gave way to less and less frequent communication until, finally, we lost track of each other altogether.

In time, I returned to the States, took up a job in a new state, and went on to graduate school. With the new location came new friends and diverse activities. Eventually, the idea of a two-week trip together into the Boundary Waters surfaced. Having paddled there in the past, I was excited to return.

We tapped the expertise of a professional guide to help us map out a special route that would take us to the most remote lakes. We covered an enormous distance in the course of the trip, never once retracing our path, and scarcely meeting others. Over a campfire one evening, I told the story of my hardy friend Bruce. In absentia he became renowned, as each camper one by one experimented with his unique portaging style. Usually, within mere feet of starting the test, the canoe would jerk, lunge back, or tip wildly to the front, crashing down with a big boom. It soon became clear the distinction of portaging sans hands would remain the honor of one man alone.

We had two glorious weeks of sunshine, paddling, exploration, and discovery. Pristine waters afforded refreshing swims after hard days of work, and the dark northern sky feted us with light shows complete with shooting stars most nights. It seemed we had the entire million acres of wilderness to ourselves...until the last portage of the last day, when out of the woods came that signature figure, arms bowed across the chest, body moving deftly, smile characteristically lighting up the face.

In awe, we watched him, much like a favorite story book character come to life, cut through the bushes and appear. Still miles from urbanization, and after five or more years, Bruce and I were reunited in this most unlikely--yet fitting--place.

Relativity: The Japan Connection
Lilah Katcher

My third cousin Dana is awesome. We can talk for hours about anything from the Harry Potter series to immigration policy. She makes a mean Japanese curry and will every now and then decide to do something like bake a batch of her grandmother's chocolate chip cookies to share with everyone. She always has a good story to share about her car falling apart on the highway, or running into someone from home while out for a walk in Istanbul.

Best of all, she's lived in my hometown for the past several years. I was always a little wistful as I enjoyed my mother's stories of growing up with her cousins nearby. My maternal grandparents were both first generation Americans with many siblings; my grandmother was one of nine children, and several of them stayed in Michigan to raise their own families. My parents moved away from Michigan before I was born. My brother and I grew up a day's drive from the closest relatives. So I was thrilled to finally satisfy that childhood longing for family close by. The fact that Dana and I have many interests in common is a bonus.

But maybe the thing that makes me most grateful is the fact that I met her at all. It might never have happened if not for Japan.

For her work, my mom had studied Japanese and traveled to Japan many times. Dana had been back in the U.S. for a year, after living in Japan for five years. As a prospective student, she came with her father to visit the university where my mom worked in the Overseas Programs office. Dana was curious about the office and stopped by with her father, but my mom was not there that day. Dana's father did not recognize my mother's married name on the door.

Dana enrolled, and her first semester went by before a Japanese student suggested that Dana go to the Overseas Programs office to talk to a person about the programs in Japan. She did, and they had a long discussion about Japan. Dana had introduced herself with her first name only. At the end of their conversation, my mother took Dana's e-mail address to follow up with some information. Later, she noticed the last name in the address.

"Do you happen to be related to any So-and-Sos from Michigan?" asked the e-mail Dana got a few hours later.

"My dad, Martin So-and-So, went to Central High School." she replied. "Did you go there too?"

"No," came the response from my mom, "but we're related."

When Dana came for dinner, I was amazed by the story of how she and my mother met. Dana was, too; she still couldn't believe it. She had been surprised enough to find someone working at her school who could speak Japanese; to then find out that person was a relative? Truly a shock.

As for me, I'm just grateful for the Japan connection that brought Dana and me together.

Samson
Bobbi Zehner

I no longer recall the age of our Brutus when he died, but he wasn't old--perhaps five or six. It was the August I turned twelve. Dad sat alone in the darkened living room for days, talking to no one. The macho man did not want to be seen crying; let alone crying over a dog. Mom and I openly shared our grief for Brutus: a lovable hundred and ten pound German boxer. Dad kept his grief tightly tucked inside the folds of his broken heart.

A year or so later, I found a newspaper ad: Good home needed for energetic boxer puppy. "Please, please, please," I implored. "Can't we just go look at it?"

When did you ever hear of just looking at a puppy? Samson, the boxer pup in question, lived with too many kids, one exhausted mother, and a father emotionally torn between his love for family and love for the pup. The father's sadness overflowed that day, as he watched Samson leave his home for ours.

As a rule, boxers make excellent family pets, with a shared loyalty to all. Sam proved to be no exception, with a noteworthy protectiveness toward Jimmy, my baby brother. Sam's preferred resting spot was my bedroom window seat. There the sun would warm his scrunched-up boxer mug, while he kept an eye on his outside world and an ear to the household within. We lived on the second floor of a large Chicago two-flat. My uncle and his family lived on the first. Sam had held his window seat vigil for several years, when one day he jumped down, barking wildly, rushing to the front door, scratching to get out. When I opened the door, he tore down the stairs. I scolded, "Samson, Sam... Come back here!" I was baffled by his behavior.

In the downstairs doorway stood my Aunt Phyllis. She was in the process of paying a delivery man, who held a pizza box in his outstretched hands. Leaping into the air, Sam knocked the guy off balance, pouncing like never before--not even for a high-octane boxer.

40

At first, I was concerned that he was protecting my aunt against an unknown intruder.

Then the overwhelmed pizza guy sputtered, "Did you say Samson?" Tears filled his eyes as he realized that this was the same boxer pup he had reluctantly surrendered to my family several years before. He and Sammy had not forgotten each other. Their devotion returned that day in the form of sloppy canine kisses and tears of human joy.

Snake Skins
Bobbi Zehner

At a time when airports still permitted escorts to the departure gate, Larry sent me off with a big bear hug and a few tender kisses. Teasingly, I said, "Are you sure there isn't anything you'd like me to bring back as a souvenir?"

He chuckled, "Well, I suppose if you have to get me something, I could use a couple of rattlesnake skins--if you come across any." Shuddering, I quickly said good-bye.

Sarah and I were bound for the comfort of dry 80-degree days, cool evenings, and no mosquitoes. Destination: Chapala, 28 miles from Guadalajara, with a population of roughly 16,000 people.

While wandering around a Chapala mercado, an open air market, I spotted a leather worker fashioning wallets, belts, and purses from animal hides. Remembering Larry's quip about the rattlesnake skins, I approached the craftsman, who spoke no English. I spoke no Spanish. Pointing to a mountain of hides, I made a hissing sound and wiggled my index finger. The craftsman rummaged deeply into the pile, coming up with a whitish colored snake skin. "Sí," I sighed, with a sad face. Circling my open palms in front of each other, I endeavored to convey...what? the shading of a rattlesnake?

"Ah, combino--sí?" the man miraculously asked.

"Sí, sí." I smiled with delight at being understood.

The next day, with Sarah's father Spence as my interpreter, I returned to the leather worker's narrow stall. I explained my desire to surprise Larry, a traditional archer, who makes his own wooden bows and arrows. Larry has hoped one day to glue a rattlesnake backing onto a long bow, in the custom of Native Americans.

The congenial craftsman said that he should have the skins in about three more days. Since I was heading back to the States sooner than that, Spence, who lived in Chapala, agreed to purchase the skins on my behalf. He would be coming to the States to visit Sarah fairly soon. Perfect. I gave Spence enough pesos to pay for the skins, confident that Larry would be pleased by my initiative.

Three months later in Madison, Wisconsin, Spence sheepishly handed back my pesos. I was baffled. He explained that he had returned to the mercado several times, with no luck. On the last occasion, the Chapala craftsman, in lieu of skins and in an effort to be helpful, proudly handed Spence a supply catalog. Not knowing where to find me in the States, he asked Spence to deliver the catalog, with his sincere apologies. The catalog was from Tandy Leather, less than two miles from my own home!

I've been told that snakes regularly shed their skins. I find myself now wishing that I, too, could shed them. Since purchasing the rattlesnake skins from Tandy Leather, I have moved them from room to room in our small, overstuffed, modest abode. They need to lay flat, undisturbed, until Larry decides to make that one special bow. By last count, it has been nineteen years.

Crossing Chilean Lakes
Vivian Fenner-Evans

In the winter of 1974, I was in southern Argentina in a small town called San Martin de Los Andes. My best friend Lorri and I wanted to travel to Chile, traversing the Andes and its many lakes. The locals said that heavy snow made such a journey impossible. We did it anyway. After crossing one lake in a boat, we found ourselves abruptly alone in remote mountains. Snow began to fall. Out of the freezing haze appeared two men, with flowing wool ponchos, on horseback.

They rode up and asked what we were doing in this forsaken forest. We explained our predicament. They said that the next lake was a trek away, and the boat crossing would not leave until 5:00 a.m.

They didn't wait for a response, and instead suddenly lifted us up onto the backs of their horses. We were both fearful and excited about where they were taking us. We rode for a little more than ten minutes and arrived at a military camp. They ushered us into a building and fed us warm tea, homemade biscuits, and berry jam. We were invited to dine with the colonel. We were so happy with the graciousness, until we were led into a room filled with about 75 soldiers, with a blaze roaring in the largest fireplace I had ever seen.

Panic beset both of us: two young American women surrounded by men in uniform without anyone knowing where we were. Our hearts were pounding, until we heard the men shout, "Canta, canta-- Sing, sing!" They wanted us to sing for them. After laughing at the preposterousness of the situation, we launched into Carol King's "I Feel the Earth Move" and "Chains," followed by every song we could recall. We sang at the top of our lungs, and then the men sang to us. They were happy to have two young women in the room, and we were delighted to be offered such warm hospitality.

The next morning, before 5:00 a.m., we were again lifted onto the horses and taken to board the boat that crossed the next lake. When we arrived in the tiny village on the opposite shore, a young man speaking English invited us to stay on his ranch. He was the son of the American ambassador and had lived in Chile his entire life. That afternoon we were once again on horseback, hunting in the forest for our dinner that night--roasted parrot!

Trading Places
Lisa Vogel West

The Buddhist teacher Lama Surya Das says, "Grace is the 'isness' of life. It's the recognition that everything is connected and sacred." I'm just starting to recognize grace in my own life. Meeting Amanda in London is an example.

In the fall of 2002, my husband Ken and I moved to London for the semester while he was on sabbatical from the University of Wisconsin-Madison. I missed my friends and hadn't connected with anyone in London yet. One Sunday morning in September, I took the subway to a service at a tiny Unitarian Church. It was my second visit. Perhaps 20 people attended on any given Sunday. I sat next to Amanda, a British woman, who had never been in a Unitarian Church before that day. She usually attended a Quaker church. As it turns out, Amanda was living alone for the semester because her husband, a college professor like my husband, was on leave for the fall semester -- at the University of Wisconsin-Madison!

Amanda and I only lived in the same city for three months, but even now, seven years later, when we get together it is as if we've always known each other.

Turning the Corner
Carolyn Stiegler

"Odd coincidences seem to happen the more you travel," says Carolyn Stiegler, from Burgundy, France. Here, she shares three of her experiences:

Many years ago, I worked in London and became friendly with Doug, a guy who worked in our subsidiary in the north of England. Four years later, married to an American and living in Brussels, I was at Brussels Airport when I literally bumped into Doug. He had been on a direct London/Zurich flight which had engine trouble and stopped off in Brussels. He should not have been there at all....

While walking through Leicester Square underground station in London, my husband suddenly ran after a gorgeous blonde. It transpired that she had been his neighbour in San Francisco three years previously.

Another time, walking along Oxford Street in London, I ran into a charming Italian with whom I had worked in Rome a few years before.

The point of this: I often wonder how many people have just turned the corner before I got there.

44

Chapter Five

Friendships link and loop and interweave until they mesh the world.

Pam Brown

Isthmus Vocal Ensemble
Robin Mozer

Robin Mozer is a proofreader, a music teacher, and a church choir director. After recently moving to Madison, she and her husband Steve were in the process of meeting new people.

Steve and I were at a party for friends we knew from Penn State, Mike and Jennell, who were now living in Madison. There I met Cara, whom I talked to for 45 minutes or so.

It was a Saturday night and I had to get to work in the morning. When people asked why we were leaving so early, I said, "Choir directors work on Sundays."

When Cara heard this, she said, "Wait, are you a soprano?" Her question came out of the blue for several reasons: 1) we were at a party with people from the communications department--music is not a major discussion starter in this group; 2) Cara is a lawyer and in the 45 minutes we were talking, she never once mentioned anything musical; 3) not all choir directors sing.

I said, "Yes."

She said, "Oh, my gosh, do you want to fill in for me? I am supposed to be in a choir this year and I can't. I'm feeling so guilty!"

I asked, "What choir?"

Cara told me briefly about the Isthmus Vocal Ensemble (IVE). The conductor is the choral director at Trinity University in San Antonio, but received his degree from the UW and previously was a conductor in Madison. He still has friends in the area, and they put together a choir of about 40 people (IVE). They rehearse intensely for three weeks. It's like boot camp--all that work for only one concert at the Lutheran Memorial Church on University Avenue.

Cara was feeling sad about dropping out at the last minute. After meeting me at the party, she introduced me to Scott, the director of IVE. Cara gave me her music. Now I'm in this fantastic choir: the director is amazingly talented, and this is the most challenging music I've sung since I arrived in Madison.

As it turned out, I discovered that in this choir were the two other voice teachers at Music by Mickey, the music school where I teach.

Haleakala
Jodi Schiro

In 2007, Jodi Schiro presented her family with a pineapple wrapped as a Christmas gift. They laughed, "What's that for? Are we going on a tropical trip or something?"

'Yes, it's a surprise," said Jodi. "We'll be spending the New Year in Hawaii together."

With little time for preparation, the finer details of their trip were left until they arrived. One of those was a Maui bus ride up to the top of Haleakala, which would then allow them to bicycle down together as a group. They were excited until they found out that the bus would leave at 4:00 in the morning. They opted to drive themselves, instead, later in the day.

Jodi, the manager of a local workout club back home, was eager to watch the sun setting over the ancient volcano's summit at almost 10,000 feet. But she also needed to find a bathroom. At around 8,000 feet, they pulled off to the side of the treacherous road where there was a modest shelter. There was only one other car in the small parking lot as Jodi scurried off to use the facility. While washing her hands, Jodi looked into the mirror and was startled to see a face she recognized. It was Mary, one of her club members, emerging from a stall. Only two women in the bathroom and they knew each other! Neither had any idea the other would be in Hawaii, much less traveling up a volcano to catch a sunset.

Dr. Jazz
Bobbi Zehner

Bonnie had often mentioned David. Because she and I had been close friends for several years, I knew that her fiancé David had died fighting a forest fire out west when they were rangers together. One particular evening, we were in a Madison restaurant discussing all-time favorite desserts. Reminiscing, I said, "Oh, I wish we could go to Dr. Jazz for ice cream." At one time, there was a Dr. Jazz ice cream parlor on Montrose Avenue in Chicago, walking distance from my apartment. I grew up in Chicago. Bonnie grew up in Lodi, Wisconsin.

Bonnie immediately said, "Yep, that Dr. Jazz place was one of a kind."

I said, "You mean Dr. Jazz in Chicago?"

"Yep," she said.

"How could you possibly know about it? It was a neighborhood joint."

She said, "David used to take me there."

"How did he know about it?" I asked.

"He grew up in that area of Chicago."

I got that tingling sensation you get when you're on the brink of discovery. "What was David's last name?" A question I'd never thought to ask, in all the years I'd known Bonnie. "Wolfson," she responded.

"Was his father a cab driver, active in the Boy Scouts?"

"Yes," Bonnie said, with eyes wide.

"Harold Wolfson," I said. "His wife was a friend of my mother's, and our families all went to school together. My uncle and Harold were Scout leaders in the same troop. When Mrs. Wolfson died, my mother, who never went anywhere without a hat, was gifted with one of Mrs. Wolfson's hats, which I now own."

Bonnie was speechless. How could we have known each other so well and not have known that this connection existed?

Dr. Jazz was the conduit--the link that leaves me wondering how many times people come into our lives without being aware that we have mutual connections? Perhaps that's partly why our skin tingles in moments like these, realizing that we could just as easily never have made the discovery.

Right Relations
Carolyn Zahn-Waxler

The theme of the Unitarian Sunday service a few weeks ago was Right Relations. At one point, we were invited into meditation, to reflect on a time when a relationship was transformed; when something had transpired to alter, enhance, and spiritually enrich our lives. While I've had these experiences, the process has usually been gradual, and I was not used to pinpointing defining moments. As it turned out, I was in the midst of one.

Before the service started, I noticed a man and woman sitting nearby. They looked to be in their late 40s or so. The woman began to talk to my husband. I did not know her, but felt as though I had known her for the better part of my life. She then introduced herself with a smile and a hug. She was Kim, the daughter of a school friend back in the 1950s, when we both lived in a small town in northeastern Wisconsin. At once I saw and heard the similarities--the eyes, the mouth, the jaw line, the voice. But it was so much more than the physical resemblance. There was a sense of openness, warmth, and vitality that reflected the animated presence of her mother, Leanne, who also now lives in Madison.

Kim told me how much her mother had cared for me and talked about me over the years. I was flooded with memories, both joyful and painful. The flowers for the services that day were in memory of Kim's father, Gary, who had died five years earlier. I'd known Gary since grade school, for their family lived just three blocks away.

Leanne had come to Sturgeon Bay from Cairo, Illinois when she was in late grade school, and we became fast friends. It seemed improbable in some ways. She was beautiful and mature, while I was a late bloomer with my nose often stuck in a book. Leanne embodied authenticity and kindness. While most of us engaged in petty fights and jealousies with our girlfriends, she took part in none of that.

Leanne and Gary met in junior high, and they were inseparable from then on, even though they came from very different family backgrounds. Toward the end of her junior year, Leanne became pregnant. Gary was a year younger and marriage was out of the question. His mother strongly pressured Leanne to go away, have the baby, and put it up for adoption. But the only option Leanne considered was to have the baby and keep it. Being an unmarried mother in those days was viewed by many as scandalous. And there was a lot of gossip in that town.

Neither Gary nor Leanne received any help from his parents or their church. It fell to her parents, a few friends, and what she mustered through tremendous conviction and courage to see her through the next few years. A few of us remained her close friends. We spent time with her during and after the pregnancy and visited her in the hospital when the baby was born.

After Gary turned 18, he and Leanne married and began family life together in Madison, where Gary was a student at the University of Wisconsin. Leanne and I saw each other from time to time, as I was a student at the UW as well, but we moved in different directions. They had two more children and remained in Madison after Gary graduated. Both became successful, respected members of the business community. It was and is a close-knit family, with mother and daughters still in business together. There were struggles too, I'm sure, but there was this overarching sense of solidarity and love that spoke volumes about right relations.

I certainly didn't go to church that Sunday expecting to meet the child born in that Algoma hospital almost half a century ago. A young mother's love protected her and kept her close, and I now know her as a part of my faith community. When we embraced at the end of the service, we both were in tears. It was a transformational experience, and it was about right relations.

Post-scripts: After submitting this story to the editors, Carolyn sent it to Leanne, who then shared it with her daughters…continuing both the connection and the concept of right relations.

Response from Leanne Starr:

You described our situation so well. It was a time in my life that made me a stronger person and many times, when approaching a difficult situation, I go back to that time and it gives me what I need to tackle the situation I'm facing.

Response from daughter Kim to Carolyn:

Nostalgia, grief, joy...these are precious things we share as "history" with the folks with whom we have "right relations." As I told Mom, I have often marveled at the beauty of our finding each other in our faith community, serendipity at its best.

From daughter Kelly to Leanne:

I have always known that I was blessed with a TRULY AMAZING Mother but never fully appreciated my blessings until I read Carolyn's words. We can only hope to be as loving to our kids as you have been to us...

A Crush Revisited
Cathy Toll

I had a terrible crush on Willie all through high school. We were in the same French class for all four years, so I had plenty of time to take in his sleepy brown eyes, jet black hair, and full, deep red lips. I daydreamed about Willie throughout the school day, and I watched for him outside his house on the way home from school. An entry in my diary from those days reveals that, "I saw Willie and his sister at the homecoming parade tonight! He looked so cute! I was so turned on." This crush was big.

High school ended, and I pretty much forgot about Willie. Imagine my shock, then, when I heard his name 25 years later at the back-to-school faculty meeting of the university where I taught. New faculty members were being introduced, and his was one of the names announced. Could it be? I was 250 miles away from Fond du

Lac, Wisconsin, where we had gone to high school. What were the odds?

The man bearing his name was not present at that faculty meeting, so I didn't get an answer to my questions that day. In fact, it took weeks before I was able to catch up with him. It was indeed Willie – now going by Will. He was still handsome; in fact, his eyes were even deeper and more appealing.

We agreed to meet for coffee and a chat. I expected that we would discuss high school and that would be it. To my surprise, Will didn't remember me from high school and didn't have much to say about those days, except to describe the pain he was in due to problems at home. However, we did have a lot to talk about, because we discovered shared research interests related to the connections between spirituality and teaching and also related to social justice practices in education. We subsequently presented papers for a conference panel, and I wrote a chapter for a book he was co-editing. He became a valuable colleague in our mutual efforts to help future and current teachers to reflect more deeply upon what mattered and how it mattered.

And, reader, you are surely wondering, so I will tell you: no, he was no longer single. This was fine with me, because I was also in a committed relationship. But we had developed a connection deeper than my high school crush.

Silver Lining
Hannah Pinkerton

In the yellowed picture, my great grandmother, Emmeline, is in front of a large brick house in Portage. She's tall, round-faced, serious, and wearing a full-length stylish dark dress, standing next to her oldest daughter, Leona. It is 1876 or a few years earlier or later. It seems a cool spring in Wisconsin, they are dressed warmly, and the leaves on the birch trees are budding. I imagine that the two women are ready for calling on neighbors. They go by buggy down the muddy streets to visit the minister's wife. Mrs. Minister is not at home, so Emmeline reaches to a small silver case hanging from her finger to remove her calling card.

She drops the card engraved with Emmeline Van Dusen into a silver dish in the front parlor. From the case she takes a small silver pencil and writes on the card. "I am sorry to have missed you. I will call later."

In the summer of 1980, I walked down the street and around the corner to where our Madison neighbors were having a garage sale. I looked through pots, pans, books and a table with old jewelry. I saw a silver case with engraving and, after bringing it into the light, I barely made out EVD etched into the top. Hmmm, strange initials. I asked what it was and where it had come from. The neighbor didn't know. It was given to her by a boyfriend who found the silver case in a pawnshop in Portage. Hmmn, could those be initials for Van Dusen? I remembered that my paternal grandmother, Floy Van Dusen, lived with her family in Portage while she was in high school, before entering the University of Wisconsin in 1891. I never got to meet her because she died a month before I was born in 1937. My middle name is Van Dusen after her side of the family. Let's see, what was her mother's name? I could check the family genealogy. I paid Felicia $20 for the silver case and took it home. In the genealogy, I found that Emmeline Van Dusen died in 1900. What had happened to her possessions, and where did the calling card case go from 1900 to 1980?

The case is silver, two and a half by five inches, with EVD etched on the front. A hinged lid opens only after a thin silver pencil is removed. A small pad of paper is on one side. Calling cards fit under a clip. There is an R&B sterling mark on the back cover. I can feel that this case belonged to Emmeline. Even though I never knew my grandmother, or my great grandmother, their stature, love of flowers, music and writing traveled down the generations to me. The silver calling card case holds their presence.

Faith
Cathy Andrews

I belong to a group of six women who call themselves A Small Christian Community. We meet every three or four weeks for faith sharing. Shirley, one of our members, developed cancer. She used to be the lab director at St. Mary's Hospital, so she knew a lot of people and had many friends. She was also one of six sisters. Over the years, as we had visited in each other's homes, we heard stories about Shirley's bond with her sisters. Going through those times with Shirley, we all grew even closer to her.

As Shirley's cancer progressed, she stopped working and a hospital bed was moved into her home. Because she was single and didn't want to be alone, different people came to stay with her at night. Saturday nights were reserved for her sisters, who lived out of town. At one Saturday night Mass, during the Kiss of Peace, my friend Val recognized Shirley's sisters, sitting right behind her. Since this was the first time all three of them had been to the Saturday evening Mass together, Val had an ominous feeling. As she greeted the sisters after the service, they told her that Shirley was close to death.

Val called, suggesting that we visit Shirley because she didn't have much time left. Fortunately, all were available at 7:00 on a Saturday night! Together, we visited Shirley one last time and felt privileged to say good-bye. Shirley died two days later.

Sometimes merely being present can be an act of grace.

Lydia's Vigil
Kate Gould

My daughter Jodie's first experience with golden retrievers was with Elvis, whom she and her husband raised from puppyhood. Elvis was a wonderful dog. When he showed signs of aging, they were able to get a puppy from one of his litter mates, hoping to have another great dog when Elvis was gone. They named the puppy Lydia. Elvis and Lydia shared the household until Elvis died.

On a recent Saturday, Jodie was awakened at 1:00 a.m. to frantic barking. Lydia's barking continued until Jodie let her outside.
At 6:00 a.m., Jodie went to the door, but Lydia was nowhere in sight... most unusual. Jodie called her name repeatedly and then drove around looking for her. Because Lydia had lost her collar the week before,

she had no ID tag. So Jodie alerted the neighbors. With no response from neighbors, she contacted the police and animal control to report Lydia missing.

Later that morning, the police notified Jodie that Lydia was fine and was at a home on the other side of the three acres of woods behind her house: an area where Jodie's family knew no one. Jodie called the people and drove over to pick up Lydia. She was full of gratitude for this family who did the responsible thing by contacting authorities...especially because Lydia had no identification.

When she went to the door, the woman invited her in and proceeded to thank Jodie profusely for Lydia's presence. The family had been up all night with their old golden retriever, who was in the last stages of life. In the wee hours of the morning, their young son looked out the window--and there was Lydia looking in! Without hesitation, the family let Lydia into their home, where she sat vigil with them until Jodie arrived. The little boy had named her Angel and wanted to keep her. Jodie explained that Lydia had a family waiting for her to come home. But they lived just on the other side of the woods and would love to have him come over to play with Lydia whenever he wanted. Jodie then looked at the dying dog, and he was a dead ringer for Elvis. Pet owners know that every animal has its own face...and this was Elvis' face!

We'll never know what drew Lydia to that home that night. Some things just can't be explained. What we do know is that Lydia gave comfort to a little boy and his family at a very sad time in their lives, and two families now know each other because of this shared experience. The family now has a new puppy, and Jodie hopes to take Lydia over to visit. We're all curious about Lydia's reaction to seeing the family again.

Fuul's Gold
Emily Standish

"You're going where?" For three months before our family trip to Syria, the questions were always the same: "Why would you go there?" By then our daughter, Sarah, had already lived in Egypt and

Jordan, and we had visited her in those places. We saw no reason to forego a trip to see her.

Arriving in Damascus, we drove through the Bab Touma gate into the Old City and stepped onto an ancient intersection of world religions, commerce, and culture. For several days we wandered streets named in the Bible, stood in awe at the mosaics in the Great Mosque, explored the market, and drank tea with shopkeepers before the haggling began.

Leaving Damascus, we moved from town to town, visiting ancient Roman ruins in the desert near the Euphrates River. Then we headed up toward the Turkish border to Aleppo to settle in for a few days. Aleppo is Syria's largest city, with a population of just over two million. It feels cosmopolitan, with vast shopping districts with windows full of women's fashions and electronics, and with sizable Armenian and Orthodox Christian communities. But not so cosmopolitan that a family of five blue-eyed blondes would be regarded as anything other than tourists. We would have to find a way to connect with local Syrians, an important part of our travel agenda no matter where we were. We always hope to unearth that lovely common humanity that nourishes and teaches us.

Our hotel fronted a pedestrian-only corridor, connected to a small grassy square ringed by jewelry shops, cafes, and produce vendors. We could wander out to sit in the winter sun with a sack of just-picked oranges or a dark, intense cup of Arabic coffee.

One afternoon, all five of us were in a tiny café on the square, a "fuul shop" that is the most famous of its kind in Aleppo because of the only thing on the menu: the creamy mixture of fava beans, tahini, garlic, cumin, lemon, and olive oil that is called fuul (pronounced "fool"). The shop, called Abu Abdo, has been operating in the same place since 1895, its recipe passed down from father to son. The most famous Syrian singers and even the Prime Minister are said to be among their loyal customers. Inside there is room for only six tables and an assortment of folding chairs. The shop opens at 7:00 A.M. every day to a long line of customers waiting to buy take-away fuul in zip-lock bags or containers from home.

But on this late afternoon at Abu Abdo, the tables were empty except for our family and one other patron sitting alone at a table near us. A ten-year-old boy took our order and another boy brought a large dish of fuul and some Cokes. On the table was a tall stack of flat bread, used to scoop up the beans and sop up the oil. The fuul was amazing: warm, garlicky, smooth.

Our family conversation centered on travel plans, accumulated questions and thoughts about Syria, and tentative talk about the current bombing of Gaza by the Israeli military.

During a pause in conversation (due to sopping and finger-licking), a voice from the next table said, "Where are you from?" It is a common enough question, and usually the asker is only wanting to know, U.S. or Canada?

"From the U.S.," I said.

"Where, in the U.S.?" This follow-up surprised us, but it still was not too unusual. The questioner often wants to know if we are from New York or California, the two places that I guess everyone on earth has heard about. The vast spaces in between, above or below, are in geographic limbo to the rest of the world.

"The West Coast, the best coast!" That from our teenager, but all eyes were now on our persistent, fuul-eating friend. We were not being cryptic; it's just that we had been through this many times before. When we mention Oregon, it requires a lot of explanation that usually ends with "near Hollywood."

"But what state on the West Coast?" He pursued us with uncommon knowledge of our fifty states. An invisible thread was pulling us toward him. Now we were definitely excited.

"Oregon." We were finally out with it!

"Well then! My wife is from Portland."

Unbelievable! In all our travels we've never met a local who has had intimate knowledge of our home state. Indeed, even among our fellow Americans, Oregon is often a blur of lumberjacks and wind surfers and food carts.

Introductions all around! Amarr told us that he and his wife, April, met in college in San Francisco in the 1980's. He had been raised in Damascus, the son of a military officer, and thus afforded the opportunity for an education abroad. April, who grew up in the suburbs, headed out of Oregon for college. They married, April converted to Islam, and they began a family. With their four children, they moved to Phoenix. They loved their Arab-American community there but felt that Amarr's roots were eluding the children. Amarr started a business based in both the U.S. and Syria; they packed up the family and moved to Aleppo.

In the café, our animated conversation was gathering steam. One of the cooks came over to listen. A customer left his place in line to join in. The two young waiters seemed astonished to hear Sarah's perfect Levantine Arabic dialect. Before long, about ten Syrian men were in the cafe, anxious for a turn to just talk with us. One shopkeeper wanted us to know that he closed up his nearby shop so that he could be part of the conversation. Amarr and Sarah carried on this exchange with the crowd for about twenty minutes, translating for the rest of us, all of us laughing, smiling, and nodding as the shop buzzed with energy.

Finally, the cooks went back to work, the customers resumed eating and ordering fuul, and the neighboring shopkeepers wandered out. We traded e-mail addresses and phone numbers and made plans with Amarr to get together again. Amarr left to return home to his family, and we counted out Syrian pounds to pay for our fuul. The cook waved his hand and shook his head. Amarr had already paid for our food on his way out.

The next evening, Amarr and April met us for dinner, and we spent the entire evening talking about, well, everything, all that we have in common. Our mutual hopes and dreams for our kids, jobs, politics, and for the world we share kept us at the table until late. April engaged each of our children in talking about their own plans and ideas. Amarr told us that he had been in the fuul stand for a quiet moment the day before, pondering how he would provide his children with the education he wants for them.

What lingered, and has now bloomed into an enduring friendship, was a connection between Amarr and April and our family. Looking across the table at April that night, in her soft white hijab and her intensely blue eyes, I was reminded again of the connection that I seek on the other side of the world in cultures about which I know very little.

In the months after meeting Amarr and April, Sarah continued the friendship from Damascus. April and I kept in touch by e-mail. Amarr provided generous advice to Sarah during her writing of a travel guide. When they were in Portland a year and a half later, they brought the whole family to see us. Their four gorgeous children romped in the yard with the dog, played in the treehouse, and learned to skateboard.

The miracle of a chance encounter in the midst of a world in constant turmoil always creates a yearning in me for more: more connection, more ways to make the planet a bit smaller. I know one thing for sure. I'll go back to Syria.

Chapter Six

How many times do people come into our lives without being
aware that we have mutual connections? Perhaps that's
partly why our skin tingles in moments like these, realizing
that we could just as easily never have made the discovery.

Bobbi Zehner

The Tumbleweed
Joyce Carey

Returning home from a marathon driving trip, my daughter Jenny and I stopped at a small farming community along Interstate 90 for dinner. By its location, there should have been a large constellation of motels and restaurants near the off ramp, but all we saw was a Perkins, whose menu we had already exhausted. Jenny had a feeling that we would find a good place to eat downtown. I wasn't so sure, expecting the usual array of bars, or with luck, a ma-and-pa eatery that served breakfast all day.

We cruised the two-block main street, and Jenny spotted the brightly lit and inviting Tumbleweed. When we entered, the few patrons were just finishing their dinners, and we had the place to ourselves. A sixty-ish woman greeted us, saying, "It's nearly eight o'clock," which we took to mean it was closing time. But no, we were welcome to stay if we wanted a pizza. I had visions of a microwaved Tombstone pizza, but it was that or Perkins' bacon-laden offerings, so we took a seat at one of the antique tables.

Our hostess brought water and menus, and Jenny engaged the woman in conversation about the pizzas. Jenny doesn't tolerate tomatoes, which pretty much limits the kind of pizza she can eat. Also, Jenny has never met a stranger. She learned that our hostess' name was Marie, and told her about having to rent a car and embark on a grueling 2000-mile drive to Oregon due to floods that grounded Amtrak. We settled on a white pizza, no tomato sauce. Marie brought big green salads, full of delicious ingredients, and heard more of our story about the week we spent at accordion camp. I usually hesitate to engage a working person in extended conversation, assuming they are busy, but Marie seemed to enjoy the talk as much as we did. After learning that we both, mother and daughter, play the accordion, Marie called her own daughter Cathy out of the kitchen. "You have to hear this," she told the younger woman, and Jenny started the tale at the beginning—the train, the long drive, accordion camp. Cathy turned to her mom, saying, "Go get the accordion!" I thought we were in for a performance, or maybe an impromptu trio.

Cathy brought out the white pizza, handmade with two kinds of cheese, artichoke hearts, spinach, mushrooms and olives—the best I ever had. She told us about her accordion, which had been her grandfather's. "It's been wrapped in a baby blanket on my closet shelf for years," she said. In a few minutes, Marie returned with the accordion—actually a melodeon, or a one-row buttonbox about the size of a small toaster. It was in remarkably good condition—a little Hohner, black with painted designs. Jenny opened it up and played "Oh Susanna," surprising me as much as it delighted our hostesses. I had no idea that Jenny knew how to play a buttonbox.

"Nobody in our family wants it or knows how to play it," Cathy said, "So I'd like you to have it."

It grew dark outside as the four of us sat and chatted. Marie and Cathy had opened The Tumbleweed a year and a half before. It is fitted out with antique tables, an eclectic mix of mismatched chairs, an antique wooden ice box, and a hand-carved sign with the name of the restaurant. They are artists: Marie painting landscapes and Cathy crafting jewelry and other items offered for sale at the register. Marie said that the freeway and Wal-Mart killed their little town. Although there are four councils working on improving and promoting the community, nothing seems to come of it. Marie and Cathy have lived in the area for twenty-two years, yet they are still regarded as outsiders. The Tumbleweed had little local support, as residents prefer to frequent the several bars on Main Street, not the fine little restaurant. They are tired, and tired of trying to make a difference, so they plan to move a few hundred miles away to a larger community and open a combination antique store and gallery.

We brought our big accordions in from the car and played a few tunes for Marie and Cathy. We all took pictures of each other and exchanged e-mail addresses. I asked for a menu to keep as a souvenir.

Then they told us they were closing. Not for the evening, but for good. We were their very last customers.

"Dinner is on the house."

I protested their generous offer, but Marie said that she knew when we came in the door that we were their final guests, and they wanted to treat us to dinner.

Jenny and I packed up the little buttonbox and our accordions, reluctant to leave the magic circle created by the four of us, mothers and daughters, in the last hour of The Tumbleweed. After hugs all around, we watched as they closed the door for the final time. There was no more driving the freeway for us that evening. We were totally overcome by our amazing encounter with two lovely, generous women, and the mysterious workings of the universe.

Richard and Solli
Linda Butler

When my husband, Richard Butler, left Chicago, he gave George Solli the phone number of our winter home in Naples, Florida. Richard said, "If you get to Naples, give me a call." Solli and Richard had both worked at O'Hare Airport for over thirty years. Solli had retired from the police department and, every morning about 3:45, he collected concession money and often had a cup of coffee with Richard.

When Solli flew to Ft. Myers, to play golf with his old friend Donna Taylor, he mentioned that he had forgotten Richard's phone number. Donna said, "I don't know any Richard Butler, but I know a Sonny Butler, who used to work for United."

Solli said, "This guy Richard just retired from United."

Donna called Sonny and said, "Hold on, I got someone here who thinks he wants to speak to you."

Solli took the phone saying, "Richard, when did they start calling you Sonny?"

Through Donna, the connection was made. As it turned out, there was another connection that no one knew about until that moment. Solli and I had grown up together! In fact, I had recently been to a Thanksgiving get-together in Chicago with old neighborhood pals, including Solli. But I had no idea that Solli had been drinking coffee with my husband for more than thirty years.

Kit in Lake Geneva
Bobbi Zehner

One weekend, my dear friend Kit invited me to the Lake Geneva cottage belonging to her sister Lynn's in-laws. Lynn and her husband had recently moved from Illinois to Ohio. The cottage was situated behind the mansions on the lake. Lake Geneva allows public access along the shoreline that runs through the property of the home owners. As we walked along the water, knowing my propensity to chatter, Kit informed me that it was not de rigeur to talk to any of the people across whose front yards we were treading. I vowed to behave and did rather well until we came upon a yard with a bouncing yellow Labrador puppy.

Without slowing my step, I asked the man reclining in a hammock, "How old is your pup?" Kit, mortified, stiffened her shoulders when she heard my voice behind her. Clearly, the puppy was no older than several months.

The man quipped, "I think he's eight or nine years old." I chuckled and commented that I, too, had a yellow lab, but I kept walking.

We had gone some distance when I said that I thought the man's voice was familiar. "Humph," said Kit. "Well, he wasn't very friendly."

"Oh, I think he was. After all, he joked about the dog's age," I countered.

So on we walked. As we circled back, I noticed the fellow was still in his hammock. Kit was leading the way, so she didn't notice when he waved to me. As I passed him, I was still trying to place his voice. Stopping abruptly, I spun around and said, "John?"

Shocked to hear his name, he leapt from his hammock. When I saw him standing, I was sure I knew him. He gasped and hugged me. Kit just gawked.

I said, "Wow, is this your parents' home?"

John said, "No, it's mine." It was my turn to gawk.

John and I had known each other years earlier in Chicago, but clearly he had become more successful in business than I had ever imagined.

The following morning, John invited us to brunch with his week-end house guests, who were old Chicago high school friends. We left a note for Lynn, Kit's sister, who was traveling from Ohio, to join us when she arrived. Lynn was pleased to see us and shocked to see John's guests: her favorite former Illinois neighbors!

New Rapport in Door County
(Author's name withheld by request)

For reasons I do not understand, my youngest brother, Joe, left his wife just before she gave birth to a beautiful son. When Joe decided to leave, he wanted none of the rest of his family to have any contact with Peg or the baby, Justin. We all liked Peg very much; she had become one of us, and we wanted to support her and Justin. When we told Joe this, he said that we were no longer a part of his family.

We expected Joe to get past his anger and re-establish a connection with the family. He did not. Six years after Justin's birth, my father had open-heart surgery. Although the rest of us gathered around my father, Joe never came to the hospital, and no one heard a word from him.

At the time, my husband and I were members of the Unitarian Society. During Dad's hospitalization, we attended a service on the topic of forgiveness. The point was to forgive people, so that they can no longer hurt you. People carry around a heavy weight when they carry around anger at another person. The service touched me and I thought of trying to forgive my brother Joe--not for him, but for me. A visualization tape led me through the forgiveness process. Part of the process was to imagine a discussion with the person you were trying to forgive. For about a week, I practiced a discussion with Joe, while I was at the hospital and while driving the car. My dad's health worsened, and the nurses called us to come to the hospital. Joe never appeared at the hospital, and he did not come to the funeral, either.

The following weekend, I decided we needed to get away. Taking off from work and school on a Friday, my husband, daughter and I headed for Door County to bike and camp. While riding on a fairly unpopulated trail, I was thinking again about forgiveness. Just then, I happened to look up--and saw the very person I had been thinking about. After six years of separation, there was Joe, riding right toward me. In shock, all I could manage to say was a weak "Hello". And then I just rode on! Catching up with my husband, I told him, "I just saw Joe!" To my surprised delight, Joe had turned around and approached us. We talked for a while, and I wished him well. Among my other very mixed feelings, I was amazed at the serendipity of the moment. Because I had been working on forgiveness, I felt genuinely happy to see him.

A few months later, Joe called my other brother and had a long talk with him. Less than a year later, Joe visited our mother, and remained in contact with her from that point on. I feel a door that was closed has been opened.

Dan and Yann in Portland
Kate Conklin Corcoran

Irene called one day in March, 2007 to tell me that Yann would be in town in April with his partner Dan, and they both wanted to see me. Through Irene, I arranged to meet them for lunch at Bluephies. I had not seen either of them since they graduated from Shabazz High School, but both were instantly recognizable: Dan blond, burly, and loud; Yann dark, lean, and fine-featured, more reserved. One of those perfectly complementary couples. We must have been quite a sight for the rest of the diners at Bluephies: a small, middle-aged woman hugging and being hugged by two huge men dressed in black leather, displaying piercings in eyebrows, ears, and lips.

I had taught both of them at Shabazz. Dan was one of my first students there, graduating in 1984; Yann graduated in 1994. They would never have known each other in Madison. Shabazz, with its nonharassment policy, was a sanctuary for gay and lesbian students, but these two were years apart in age and came from very different backgrounds. Dan had lived on his own and supported himself through his last year of high school. After graduation, Dan took off for Portland, Oregon, not returning to Madison until the week of my meeting with them nearly twenty years later.

Yann's parents, Irene and Paul, were both gentle, loving people. While they were concerned about Yann's future, they supported the choices he made even when they did not agree with them, as when he decided not to go to college. Yann, too, moved to Portland, Oregon after graduation. At the time, Portland and San Francisco were Meccas for many Shabazz students who were ready to leave Madison behind. They were good, progressive cities to move to if you wanted a new start but also some kind of support network.

Dan was a waiter at a large, upscale restaurant in Portland. Walking down the street on his way to work one day, he noticed Yann, the good-looking waiter serving people at the tables outside a popular café. That day, Dan only paused long enough to know he would remember that waiter. After that, Dan made a point of always passing the café on his way to or from the restaurant. Soon enough, Yann had noticed him, too, and they began to nod at each other and say hello.

Dan hadn't made an approach because he could tell that he was much older than Yann. One day, though, Yann left work later than usual, just as Dan was passing by. They fell into step and into conversation. In the initial exchange of who-are-you's, they discovered that they had both attended Shabazz. Such an unlikely synchronicity in a city of 545,000 people –and coming from Shabazz graduating classes of about 25 people--convinced each of them that their meeting was destined.

The Hawk
Nancy Jesse

The morning after my mother's death, my brother and I made funeral arrangements in our home town. We stopped to comfort my cousin, Laurie, who lives across the street from my parents' old house. Laurie was a close friend of Mom's and was shaken by the news of her death.

As we were sitting at the kitchen table, talking about Mom, Laurie suddenly looked up and said, "Oh, my gosh, I've never seen that before."

I turned around slowly and saw a little hawk, perched on a tree, looking in our window. It gazed at us for a long time before flying toward the window. Then it abruptly turned and flew in the direction of Mother's old house. When I first saw the beautiful bird, the word "Mother?" popped into my mind. It was only later, when I told my husband about the hawk, that I recalled that Mother's maiden name, Meisegeier, in German, means a small bird of prey.

Karma
Bobbi Zehner

With a 40%-off coupon in hand, I dashed to Half Price Books, prepared to zip through the store and get back home in time for dinner. Lately, I've been on a recycling kick, hunting down favorite titles to give to loved ones. Scanning the shelves, my eyes seized upon Sylvia Boorstein's *It's Easier Than You Think: The Buddhist Way to Happiness.* Holding it tenderly, I stroked its cover with familiar affection. What great luck! This book, the one I have given most often, was not in this very store two weeks ago. A hard copy, which new would probably cost twenty bucks, now could be mine for three dollars and fifty-nine cents. Surely this was karma at work.

Opening the book, I saw an inscription from October of '96, to Lynnae and Andy, which read:

"Simple, yet profound is how I'd describe Boorstein. I love being able to share her wisdom with you trusting you'll pass it on as well.

The wisdom, that is--the book is a keeper! Thanks for all the joy you've brought my way. Love, B."

B? That's me! Lynnae and Andy? That's my goddaughter and her husband, who live in Oak Park, Illinois. I bought Boorstein's book for them in Madison, Wisconsin, and now I'm buying it again in Madison, Wisconsin--the very same copy! I figure it wasn't such a keeper, after all.

To my scribed words, someone had added "10/31/04-To Ryan." Guess Ryan didn't think it was much of a keeper, either.

Standing amid the stacks at Half Price Books, in February of 2006, I found myself laughing. It's been said that books are gifts that keep on giving every time they're opened. Since Buddhism was the subject of this particular text, it occurred to me that my inscription should not have read "...the book is a keeper," but rather:

"...I love being able to share her wisdom with you, trusting that you'll pass it on, as well. That goes for the book, too, because books are meant to be shared."

How's that for insight deferred? Through happenstance, the lesson has become mine; the one I didn't get the first ten times I read the book! But who is Ryan--a friend of Lynnae and Andy's? Did his godmother buy my book at a yard sale in Oak Park, especially for him? And how did it find its karmic way back to Madison and into my hands?

My Lifelong Friend
Neil Amber

When I was young, travelling off the beaten trail, friends would come and go. I was savouring each day, and it was a given you'd likely never meet up again. Even years later, while looking over the back pages of a journal--names and addresses, places to visit, books to read, Hindi alphabet and so on--I cannot recall the names or faces of most of the people. The one exception is Grant Hughes from Invercargill, my lifelong friend.

It's funny how different memories work. Grant was certain we first met on a long train trip. Yet in the first image I recall, he's wearing a white cotton shirt and pants, sitting inside a mosquito net doing pranayama, a yogic breathing practice, at an ashram in Andhra Pradesh.

We next met up, surprisingly, at an obscure ashram north of Madras, in a tiny mudbrick village called Jellulamudi. The ashram revolved around a woman who was seen as the embodiment of the divine mother, Jellulamudi ama. She didn't speak, but from inside her colourful sari, she radiated love from her entire being: true motherly compassion. When I met her, there was Grant, sitting at her feet for another life lesson. I stayed on for two weeks; he apparently bedded in for three months.

After completing an extensive mountain trek in Nepal, I was having a late lunch at the Lost Horizon Tibetan restaurant back in Kathmandu, the only customer. I had just collected over 20 letters from the Post Ristante in the post office and was reading news of old friends and family over a plate of vegetable thukpa. While twirling my fork around some noodles, I looked up at the entrance--and there was Grant, looking stunned to encounter me again. He'd just arrived in town and was also out for a late lunch. In a city of dozens of restaurants, he had selected the Lost Horizon. Perhaps the stone carved Buddhas out front drew him towards the door. So serendipitous it seemed. We entered into conversation as though we'd arranged a meeting in advance.

Grant and I spent many days walking in nearby hills, finally getting to know one another as more than just passing acquaintances. Each of us was unclear regarding where to travel next. When you're sitting on a Himalayan hill, gazing at jagged snow peaks, you have this sense of boundless freedom to choose any direction to journey. It's an incredible feeling, but you can be quite confused. I encouraged Grant to visit the Gharwali Mountains in north India where major rivers have their sources and pilgrims hike the steep tracks to ancient shrines.

I had just read in a letter of my grandmother's passing and that she'd left me $1,000. This was an impressive sum of cash, considering my frugal budget. I decided to travel into Thailand and down to Indonesia. Upon landing in Bangkok and locating a suitable hotel room, I decided to explore the nightlife. I had spent over a year in India and Nepal, in places where discos and nightlife did not exist. That night I entered a disco club in the Grace Hotel frequented by expats, GI's and travellers. Since the club was so crowded, I approached a table with an empty chair, preparing to order a beer--and then focused on a young Thai woman sitting in Grant's lap! Having known only his philosophical or spiritual side, to me this seemed totally out of character. But Grant seemed equally immersed in this element, so completely comfortable in his skin. We spent a modest amount of time together then, but I had places to go, and he was never in a hurry!

Some months later, I finally reached Bali and settled into a homestay in a hilly arts village in view of the volcanoes. After unpacking, I was reading in the courtyard, and in walked Grant! By now I was completely flummoxed; it was obvious I couldn't shake off this man. So we spent the next few weeks together. At night we'd sit beside rice terraces for hours, listening to frogs croaking, sharing our stories and our personal philosophies. In the day we'd roam through the morning market, savouring black rice pudding, or eating tasty rambutans and mangosteens. Old women smiling through their betel-stained orange teeth, the constant smell of clove scented cigarettes they call Kretecs. Living day to day, in the moment, with no bills to pay, no worries. At a full-moon ceremony in the monkey forest temple, with hours of gamelan music and a shadow puppet theatre, the Wyang Kulit, we decided to stay in touch, to even spend time together back in New Zealand.

Which is what we did. His homeland was on the mountainous south island, with less than a million people. The land was vast, seemingly deserted after the streets of Asia. He and I and another close friend spent weeks planting potatoes as a winter crop up on the highest steep hills above the line of frost. At lunch we'd gaze across the valley to the long white ridges of the Southern Alps, trying to make sense of our years in Asia and wondering how we could integrate back into the western way of life. Our hearts had been deeply touched by so many faces, by so many experiences. So much that we had seen, smelled, tasted was absent from the life in New Zealand. There were a lot of sheep, but no peasant herders. It was kind of lonely. We felt somewhat alienated at the time and just wanted to live outside of society and try out a new way of life. Though it was to be only a phase, at the time when a few families formed a community along the remote west coast, it felt like just the right place to live. Te Whenua, Maori for 'Of the Land', was reached only at low tide by foot, hiking over rocks for over an hour south of the Little Whanganui River. It was hilly and wild, the surf pounded, and it often rained for days on end. With tall tree ferns and neecal palms, it felt nearly unmapped and so remote, with enormous potential of a simpler lifestyle.

I found out soon for myself, though, that I did in fact have a lot to learn still out in the world and moved on. Grant actually lived there for many years, where he helped birth his only daughter and raised her in a rustic cabin. He, too, discovered eventually that he was in a sense escaping the world and hiding from perhaps a duty to give something back to a world that had given so much to him. We both, though, were to be naturalists for life and chose work in organic farming and land stewardship. Years later, when I migrated to Australia with my partner and young children, Grant became a part of our family, visiting most years. Truly marvellous our friendship became after such a mysterious beginning. How nice to be aging with my lifelong friend.

Boomer
Kate Gould

In 1995, my husband, Bob, and his mountain climbing partner, Ken, were involved in a terrible accident that left Bob with a traumatic brain injury and literally tied to the side of a mountain. Ken, whose nickname was Boomer, did everything correctly after the accident and was able to get the help needed to save my husband's life. While Bob was recovering in the hospital, Boomer gave my husband his favorite hat, a painter's hat with Felix the Cat on it. Bob kept Boomer's hat nearby during two months of rehabilitation. We have that hat to this day. Sadly, only eight years later, Boomer suffered a heart attack and died. The loss was overwhelming for us, but in one small way Boomer is still in our lives.

We've always had a cat in the house and are drawn to black and white ones—much like Felix. Though we weren't in the market for another cat, a funky-looking black and white adult male was living at our veterinarian's office and looking for a home. We decided to adopt him. We have always named our cats after book characters or favorite people and had decided to name the cat Jake, after my dad. One night it occurred to me that the Humane Society had approved our application on December 28th, the anniversary of Boomer's death. And we had picked him up on January 3rd, the anniversary of Boomer's funeral. I asked my husband if it would be okay to name the new cat Boomer, and he thought it was a great idea.

We knew we'd made the right decision when the paperwork from the Humane Society arrived two weeks later. Boomer had been found and turned in on July 15--the anniversary of Bob and Ken's climbing accident eleven years earlier.

Chapter Seven

Synchronicity is a reality for those who have eyes to see.

Carl Jung

"Is This the Party to Whom I am Speaking?"
Judy Meyer

Linda and I had known each other for about six months before we realized we both worked for the UW Extension. She was dating a friend of ours, and we had met her through him. We were sitting at the Village Bar one evening, just talking with a group of friends, when I heard her say her last name. It sure rang a bell with me.

"Where do you work?" I asked.

She said, "UW Extension. Why?"

When I told her my last name, we both yelled out "WISLINE." This was the network I coordinated. Here Linda and I had been talking on the phone, scheduling teleconferences for four years, and never realized our connection until that evening.

Laughing Out Loud
Rebecca Gilbert

My sister gave me a book when I was visiting: *Female Nomad and Friends*. She said she had liked it and I would, too. "You can take it on the bus," she said.

I did like the book, and when I read Bobbi Zehner's story, I laughed. Then I read the end note, about her interest in collecting stories of coincidence. Wow, I thought, things like that happen to me all the time! Like... like.... darn! I couldn't think of one. I racked my brain, and still couldn't think of one. Slightly frustrated, I turned the page, and the next story was by Lily Morris. I know Lily Morris! Probably not the same one. Resisting the urge to turn to the end note, I began to read. Within two sentences I knew it was the same Lily, a young lady whom I have admired for years, whose work I respect and whose parents I know. So there you have it.

One more crazy old lady laughing out loud on the bus.

The Old Friend
Elaine Kelly

Dennis was attending a luncheon seminar in Albuquerque hosted by a friend who was a financial planner. The luncheon was held in the banquet room of a local restaurant. The friend is an expert in his field, but his presentation can be dry. Dennis soon tired of sitting and listening to the talk and got up and went to the back of the room. Standing against the wall, he looked out the back doorway and saw a man wave at him. Dennis was amazed. The man waving at him was Eddie, his best friend from high school in East Moline, Illinois. Eddie happened to be on vacation, passing through Albuquerque. He and his wife had stopped in the restaurant for lunch ... and had run into Dennis, whom they had not seen since the high school reunion 24 years earlier.

Independent News Company
Bobbi Zehner

After forty-plus years, a surprising phone call came from Norman, my birth father. Talking with him, I learned that he had four other offspring, all younger than I: Becky, Judy, Norma, and Philip. In a subsequent phone conversation, Norman said that he had informed his family about my existence and that I should not be surprised if one of them contacted me.

Norma was the first to call. She had recently moved to Florida from New Jersey. I quickly flew out for a visit. She was a talker--just like me-- the first of many similar traits we discovered. We were both left-handed, had TMJ, basal cell spots, and a slightly offbeat sense of humor. The comparisons seemed endless, as we yakked and laughed well into the night.

The next morning over breakfast, we continued following the threads of our lives. Norma was raised in Alaska. I was born in California and grew up in Chicago. Almost offhandedly, I asked, "When you lived in New Jersey, where did you work?"

"In New York City, for Independent News Company, a magazine distributor. Most people have never heard of them."

"Never heard of them?" I blurted. "I know them. They were bought out by Warner Communications." I got that eerie feeling that rides the cusp of discovery. "Who did you work for?"

"Sy Rosenzweig."

"Sy Rosenzweig!" Ten years earlier, while working for a publisher in Chicago, I had routinely called Independent News Company, twice a week, for sales data. Unbeknownst to either of us, Norma, my own half-sister, was the woman in Sy Rosenzweig's office relaying the information.

Forest Hill Cemetery
Ardis Erickson

In September, Ardis and her husband spent an evening visiting Ardis' sister in Eau Claire, Wisconsin. Following a good night's rest, the three of them ate an early breakfast at Perkins and headed over to Forest Hill Cemetery. Their mission: to bring home the flower basket which they keep on the family graves during the warmer months of spring and summer.

At exactly 7:45 on this gloomy morning, they saw the figure of lone woman walking towards them. As she drew closer, Ardis realized it was her niece, Ann--the niece she doesn't get to see very often, because Ann lives in Minneapolis, Minnesota.

Ann had parked her car in Eau Claire and walked about a mile and a half to the cemetery. Unbeknownst to her aunts, she had driven to Eau Claire expressly to visit her mother's grave at the family site. The relatives were thrilled to see each other on that dark, misty morning as they gave Ann a lift back to her car.

At Doretha's Diner
Tenia Jenkins Powell

After a lengthy but ultimately unsuccessful marriage, I had no desire ever to remarry. But I never ruled male companionship out of my life. I do have a lifelong reputation to live up to, after all. Some call me a natural born flirt. I prefer to describe myself as sassy. While I wasn't exactly looking for that perfect someone, I was definitely still looking.

Though I grew up in southern Mississippi, I have lived in Madison, Wisconsin since I was eighteen years old and a freshman at the University of Wisconsin. Though my career, sons, and grandchildren are all in Madison, I spend most holidays and at least a month each summer visiting my mother, sisters, and the rest of my family in Ruth, Mississippi.

One steamy Friday night in mid-July of 2002, I decided to pick up some fish dinners from a favorite place--Doretha's Diner in Summit, about twelve miles away. Going out the door, I teased my mother: "I'm going to get us dinner--and find a man for you and one for me."

On this warm summer night, I was in no hurry. I sauntered down the street in Summit and into Doretha's--and there HE was. He was tall, handsome, and I caught him looking at me. I walked right up to him and began a conversation, realizing that I only had a couple of minutes to make my move.

If you live in Small Town, Mississippi, the important thing to learn is where someone works. As we waited for our dinners, we talked about our jobs. I told him my name, but I didn't catch his last name. I did learn, though, that he worked as a USDA inspector at the local chicken plant, where my sister-in-law Cynthia also worked. I also checked out his left ring finger. No wedding ring or giveaway light line. But when his order arrive --three dinners--I felt certain that the other dinners must be for his wife and child. So I backed off a bit, tuned down the flirtation vibe, and kept the conversation light.

When he left, he said, "See you around." I didn't think it was any more than a conventional exit. Still, I was intrigued enough to ask Cynthia if she knew a Dywane.

Cynthia asked, "Oh you mean that good-looking Dywane Powell? I know he's not married."

"Is there a girlfriend or boyfriend? He had three dinners."

Cynthia said that Dywane was recently out of a relationship; so he was available but a hard one to catch. "All the women in the plant are after him. He just ignores them."

I said, "But I can run fast, and I believe I can catch him."

But, because of the three dinners, and some old-fashioned, ingrained beliefs about whether a woman should chase a man, I put the incident to rest, saying, "Well, he knows how to contact me."

When I was back in Mississippi, in December of 2003, Cynthia called. "There's someone here who would like to talk to you."

An unfamiliar male voice said, "Hello. My name is Dywane Powell. Do you remember me?"

My reply: "No, I sure don't."

"Remember I met you in Doretha's in Summit?"

After a calculated pause, I said, "Oh yes, I remember you now."

We spoke for a short while, and Dywane asked, "Mind if I call you sometime?"

It had been a year and a half since we had first met, and he hadn't made any attempt to contact me. Before I said yes, I wanted to know why he waited so long. He said he had often asked Cynthia about me, but never while I was in town. Also, he was in the U.S. Army Reserves and had been called up to train soldiers in response to the 9/11 terrorist attacks. He had been away from Mississippi from September of 2002 until the spring of 2003.

Cynthia had placed our only phone call, so Dywane didn't have my number and perhaps felt reluctant to ask her for it. He is a very reserved man, almost shy, but he managed to call every Jenkins in Ruth, Mississippi looking for me. And that was a lot of phone calls--half of Ruth's population is named Jenkins. Finally, from a cousin, Dywane tracked down my mother, and I happened to be at her house when he called. We didn't meet, though. I decided to play it slow; if he was really interested, he would call me in Madison.

I was only back in Madison a couple of days when he called.

That flirtation over fish at Doretha's Diner turned into something deep and permanent. In June 2008, we jumped the broom and entered into our new life together, which we divide between McComb, Mississippi and Madison, Wisconsin.

Not a Dog Person
Carrie Link

"Ever think of getting this boy a dog?" asks the kindly behavioral/ developmental pediatrician. We've been coming to see him for twelve and a half of Wil's fourteen years of life. He spins in his green leather chair, looks up at us from over the tops of his glasses, and waits for a response.

"No, we're not getting Wil a dog. I know who would take care of a dog, and I cannot possibly take care of one more living creature."

"Yes, but the right dog would give 90% and take 10%. Just promise me you'll think about it. Wil needs someone to be responsible for. Wil needs a buddy. Wil needs a best friend. Wil needs a dog. Get a Lab."

"But what about the hair?" I say. "I hear the hair is everywhere. I'm not good with everywhere."

"If you're worried about the hair, get a Labradoodle," he simply says. "They don't shed, they're smart, and they are very relational, like labs."

"I promise to talk to my friend who has both a child with special needs and a Labradoodle," I say.

I walk out of there with no intention of getting a dog.

Next day I run into my friend, Candace, at the grocery store. "Wil's doctor wants me to get Wil a Labradoodle," I tell her. "I have a Labradoodle," she says. I had not known this. We talk and talk-- and then in walks Patty, who has the boy with special needs and a Labradoodle. Of course she does.

"Patty! I just told the doctor yesterday that I would talk to you about getting a dog for Wil. Can't believe you just walked in!"

Patty laughs. Candace laughs. They believe in synchronicity, and so do I. What you put out there to the universe takes on a life of its own. We talk about Labradoodles and Candace says, "Labradoodle

Angels--go to their website and check them out. That's where we got ours."

"Yeah, they're great," Patty says, "but they only have puppies. I know you, Carrie. You aren't a puppy person. If you can get over the hair thing, you should talk to Claire. She places retired and 'career change' guide dogs." Now Claire and I are not good friends, but our kids went to the same grade school and one of hers is in high school with my daughter. We're neighbors. We're in each other's orbits. We have a lot of mutual friends.

"Sounds good," I say. "I'll talk to Claire." I make a mental note to contact Claire in roughly six months. Maybe a year. Give us all some time to think about it. No rushing in. These things take time. We've never had a dog; we're certainly not running out and getting one, just because the man who's steered us right for over a dozen years tells us to!

I go home and Google "Labrador Angels". The first puppy I see is one named Mary. I am a big Mary lover. Mary, as in the mother of God. The feminine face of God. The female divine. That Mary.

I take it as a sign. A sign to be ignored, because we are not getting a dog.

Two days later my husband, Stan, and I are debating whether or not we want to go to a fundraiser. Of course the answer is no, we do not want to go. We want to stay home and watch bad TV and go to bed at 9:00. But dear friends of ours, Jim and Kristen, have asked us to join them. And so we put on better clothes, freshen up, and head out the door.

Barely two steps into the building, I hear, "Carrie! I understand I'm supposed to talk to you about getting a retired guide dog for Wil!" It's Claire. Of course it is. Our paths never cross, but tonight they do. Later I ask Patty why it took her so long to get to Claire. She says, "Carrie, I swear, I hadn't seen her in a year. She knocked on my door the very next day after I ran into you at the grocery store."

Stan, Jim, and Kristen are off getting drinks and I cozy up to Claire. "Now, tell me, why or why should we not get a dog?" I tell her about Wil's special needs, that he's on the Autism Spectrum. I mention that Wil has ADHD, and I need one more noisy, needy, hyper thing around the house like I need a hole in the head. I chatter on and on in some vain hope that I'll ruin all chances we have of ever getting a dog from Claire. I paint our picture as dark as possible. Because. Because I already know what she's going to say before the words spill from her broadly smiling mouth.

"I hate to tell you, but I have the perfect dog for you right now."

Claire goes on to tell me all about Flicka, a six-year-old they retired early because she was showing physical signs of stress. Flicka, the most mellow dog on the planet. Flicka, the one they could place a hundred times over but because she's so amazing and has so much left to give, they are looking for just the right fit: a family with children, ideally with a special needs child. Flicka, the angel. Flicka.

"Let me think about it, Claire," I say, my eyes glancing over to find Stan in the crowd.

"Sounds great," Claire says. "Why don't you give me a call next week if you're interested?"

We part; I make my way over to Stan, Jim, and Kristin. "That was Claire," I say, "She has the perfect dog for us. Right now."

"Claire? With Guide Dogs? We've adopted two of her dogs," says Jim, while Kristen nods wildly with enthusiasm.

Of course they have.

That night I can't sleep. I want that dog. I must have that dog. No other dog on the planet will do. There is a scarcity of perfect dogs, and I must have that one. I can hardly contain myself until Monday morning, when I call Claire the very first thing. She's not there. I leave a message. Then another one. Then an e-mail. Then I send one to her home e-mail address, too.

I hear from Claire on Tuesday. Turns out she has Mondays off. Turns out she has not placed Flicka yet. Turns out Flicka is ours if we want her.

We want her.

We have her – two weeks from the moment the doctor suggested we get a dog.

Chapter Eight

The afternoon knows what the morning never suspected.

Swedish Proverb

Loose Lips
Bobbi Zehner

No longer working full time, I was free to pop into my local exercise club almost any time of day I chose. A woman first known only to me as Ann had a similar habit, so over the years we chatted quite a bit about our personal lives, while working the exercise circuit together.

I might see Ann once or twice a week, and then not again for a couple of weeks, when we generally continued the thread of our personal sagas. I knew, for example, that while she and her husband were both retired, he returned daily to his old company out of sheer habit. Ann had expressed bewilderment at his devotion, although coupled with her joy at having him out of the house.

My spouse, Larry, had spent a rough couple of years in and out of the hospital; Ann inquired about his ever-changing progress each time we met. Eventually, Larry healed and returned to work. Like Ann, I was relieved to have my house to myself.

Ann traveled, I traveled, and so we didn't see each other for several months. When we did, one of Ann's first questions was, "How's your husband?"

"Oh, Ann," I lamented, "He has decided to retire and I don't know how I'm going to handle it."

"Boy, do you ever have my sympathy, but I thought your guy was too young to retire," Ann replied.

"Ah yes, but he was offered an early buy-out and, along with 13 other people, he's taking it."

Triggered by the word "buy-out," Ann asked, "Where does he work?"

When I said "Forest Products Laboratory," Ann gasped. "What is Larry's last name?"

When I told her, she gasped again, "Oh my god, all this time we've been talking about someone I know, and he's your husband?"

As it turned out, not only did she know Larry, but so did her husband. For many years, all three of them had worked at the same place at the same time. Now what had my loose lips wrought? Frantically,

I tried to recall how much I had shared about Larry, hoping it was all good.

Face to Face
Nandi Hill

I am the New Mexico state representative for ICTC (The International Center for Traditional Childbearing). Keesha is the new state rep in Illinois. She and I have become friends on Facebook, but her profile pictures are either a side view, or with her hair covering her face.

On the first day of our family vacation in Chicago, my sister Melissa and I took the children to the Lakefront. When we were leaving, the parking lot was still very full. While we waited for our children to change their clothes, a woman in a car drove up and noticed that we were getting ready to pull out.

The driver asked, "Are you leaving?"

I said, "Yes, after my daughter is finished getting dressed."

Then we both looked at each other like we knew something was different. Before I could say anything, she said, "Are you Nandi?"

I said, "Wait... are you Keesha?"

Intuitively, we recognized each other; I got goose bumps all over my arms. Come to find out, Melissa herself had been trying to reach Keesha for help with some projects. And she, too, had never met or seen Keesha. So it was a moment that will stay with us forever.

Arlington, Iowa
Ardis Coffman

At a recent meeting in Madison, Sandi Bassett mentioned visiting parents in northeast Iowa. Turns out she is from the same tiny town my late husband was from. I mentioned this to my brother-in-law and he said, "You now know .001 percent of the people in Arlington, Iowa."

There are only 600 people in the town. So, with Sandi and my brother-in-law's family of five, I know six of them.

Jim's Signal
Mary Moen

When my husband Jim and I retired, we downsized to a condominium. Sadly, just a few months later, Jim died in our new home. I was going through a bad time, wondering if I could handle everything alone. One night, I was in my kitchen crying for him, missing his arms around me. Suddenly, I felt those two arms pull me close, as if he was standing right next to me. It was very comforting.

After that experience, I had more evidence that Jim was still in my life. When I started dating again, I connected with Bill, whom I had known as a teenager. The first time he came to my condo, suddenly one of my phones rang. The ringing came from the small den that Jim had made into his office--but not from the other phones in my home. I think Jim was trying to warn me that Bill was all wrong for me and, sure enough, Jim was right! Thank heavens I caught on in time--a relationship with Bill would have been a disaster.

A Glimpse into the Future
Shoshauna Shy

I met my husband Jim in 1978. I was living in a communal household; Jim moved into one of the rooms that had been vacated. I was slated to move out soon--but our whirlwind courtship changed my decision to depart. Jim moved in on a Sunday, took me out for my first driving lesson on Wednesday, and then we spent the night together that Friday. This was 33 years ago. We've been spending our nights together ever since.

Actually, we almost had met two years before. When we compared notes about the summer of 1976, we learned that we were both in the San Francisco Bay Area traveling alone at the very same time. One evening in June, I was hitchhiking on a freeway from Mill Valley to Sausalito. Jim was driving the same freeway. As we compared our summers, he realized that he had seen me hitchhiking and had even considered stopping--but considered it a few seconds too late!

Of course, we both couldn't help but wonder how differently our lives would have turned out if we'd made each other's acquaintance on that freeway.

The Stranger
Elaine Kelly

My mother told us of the time, either during or shortly after World War II, when our family was returning to our home in Shell Lake, Wisconsin after visiting relatives in Minnesota. It was winter and snowing; the desolate, country road was snow-covered and slippery. Suddenly, as my father braked, the car slid toward a ravine. We had a flat tire. Our spare had already replaced another tire a short time before. Furthermore, spare tires were in short supply because rubber and tires were needed for the war-time effort.

While our family sat huddled in the car, a second car pulled up beside us. The driver asked my father if anything was wrong. My father told him about the flat tire and having no spare. The stranger told him that he just happened to have two spare tires in his trunk. After my father replied that he had no money, the man asked where my father worked and said that he would come by later to be paid.

Because my father suffered from rheumatoid arthritis, it would have been difficult for him to change the tire in the cold. The stranger changed the tire for us and went on his way. He later stopped by my father's work and was paid for the tire.

My mother told this story many times, with gratitude and amazement at the grace and synchronicity.

Traveling Place Mats
Carolyn Zahn-Waxler

Terry owns Spin, a yarn store located in the former Branch Bank of Sturgeon Bay, Wisconsin. The building has been beautifully refurbished. Terry had known my father when she worked at the main bank as a young woman, but I only met her five years ago. From there, she went into real estate; still later she started a successful restaurant, the Inn at Cedar Crossing. After a while she sold the Inn to open the yarn shop, which also serves as a community center for women who enjoy socializing while they knit and crochet.

Terry and I have several common interests. Probably the most compelling one has to do with ways to foster well-being and spiritual growth. One December I'd invited her out to my home for lunch to show her our labyrinth and council ring. We never got outside, because of heavy rains, but we talked for hours.

As we were finishing lunch, she said, "You know, these place mats look just like those we had at the Inn."

My mother had given them to me almost 20 years before. They were soft rose in color, with matching napkins. They had worn well over the years, suggesting that they might have been designed for utilitarian use.

Terry continued to stare. It wasn't just that they looked similar to her; they looked identical--like they had come from the Inn. She then asked, "By any chance, did the place mats come with the house?" At first it seemed like an odd question. Ordinarily the question "Does it come with the house?" refers to large items like kitchen appliances, or a washer and dryer--but place mats?

Suddenly, I realized what was going through her mind. Terry knew that we had bought the house from a couple who lived in the country. Years earlier, the wife had worked as a chef at the Inn. At some point the place mats were probably changed, and people who worked there took the old ones.

Here's what I think happened: The husband's mother, Phyllis, had lived next door to my mother. The wife probably gave quite a number of the place mats to her mother-in-law, who in turn gave quite a number of them to my mother. My mother gave them to me. I must have had close to 20 at one point. Since neither Phyllis nor my mother cooked or entertained much in their later years, they would have had no need for the place mats. So they cycled back to serve Terry once more, decades after she'd purchased them. Was it mere happenstance or coincidence? Or is there something about the way we form personal connections that heightens the likelihood of such synchronicities?

Meeting Ravi Khanna
Neil Amber

We strive in life to understand everything, don't we? Yet there is a certain unnamable mystery that can tantalize, even suddenly surprise us. Perhaps it seeks to unravel and defy our desire to be in control. Did you ever wonder what the expression "perfect timing" really meant? I thought about it long and hard after meeting Ravi Khanna.

Let's enter the story on a freeway entrance in New Mexico. I pulled over to give a lift to a tall, thin man named Cha Chi from Peru. Such a warm smile you'd trust straight away. It's a long drive from New Mexico to Boston, and we talked a lot. Soon Cha Chi described an Indian man he had worked with named Ravi Khanna. I felt chills all over as I instantly realized that we both knew the same man. I had plenty of time to tell Cha Chi my story, which began on a long train trip in North India in 1975.

Two American women I'd chanced upon told me that when I stopped off in a village called Brindavan, the fabled birthplace of Lord Krishna, I should look up Ravi Khanna at the Hanuman temple. He would take care of me. Now, there are reputed to be over 5,000 temples in this town, which hovers between myth and history. However, late at night, following adequate directions to this temple of the monkey god, I approached a man. I asked where I could find Ravi, only to hear that I was speaking to him! He was humble and gracious, and he housed and hosted me for two weeks. Each morning we'd sit at a market tea stall, sip chai, and eat thick buffalo yogurt with bananas. He'd translate the Hindi gossip he heard around him and would tell me stories about his guru, Neem Keroli Baba.

Ravi explained how the guru had been thrown off a train once for not having a ticket. The train stood still for hours until the conductor finally came down and bowed to this maharaja. The name of the town being Neem Keroli, he adopted that name and decided to stay there for many years, gaining a big following. People such as the famed Ram Dass (who wrote the book *Be Here Now*) came to spend time with this man, who was seen daily, wrapped in a blanket, exuding ultimate inner peace.

Yet it was the simple and kind man named Gyan Shym Das, to whom Ravi introduced me, who really touched my heart in a way I couldn't have imagined. He and his wife lived in a narrow, dank alley. For the last 35 years, she had taken care of him while he spent each day caring for two black basalt deities of Krishna and Radha: cleaning them with coconut water, adorning them with flowers and incense, and praying to them. His devotion was the epitome of selfless service. Gyan had once been employed for years, with great status, by the regional Maharaja to communicate news to the Viceroy/ Governor General of the British Raj. After weeks in the hospital with malarial fever, a dream or vision opened his eyes to lord Krishna. Upon leaving the hospital, Gyan went straight to a park in Brindavan. Under a certain tree, he started digging a ditch and uncovered these two deities that he had seen dancing in his dream. This event changed his life fully, and he'd cared for and worshipped Radha-Krishna ever since. Though most people would consider this man mad, I was sufficiently impressed and always have remembered Gyan Shym with utmost awe.

Soon I bid farewell to Ravi, extremely enriched, and continued my travels for another five months. When my visa was expiring, I rode a train for 40 hours to the city of Varanasi/ Benares, on the Ganges River, on route to Nepal. I'd had a difficult trip, sleeping very little on the floor of the coach for two nights, and arrived late afternoon. A bicycle rickshaw man cycled me to a hotel, carried my rucksack up to the room, and lit up a pipe of his personal local herbs. I drifted into a daze on my bed. Although I was quite exhausted, an unavoidable urge pulled me up to go and see the river for sunset. After all, it was my first visit to Benares, and I'd read so much about its holy nature, the renowned 'City of Shiva'. I wandered down narrow crowded streets, past a sea of faces, scents and stenches, following directions. I finally reached the ghats, the stone steps leading down to the river. I nearly walked right into a man standing there. When I focused, I recognized my friend Ravi Khanna! Wow! How could this be? I thought to myself. So astonishing that in a city of over three million people, where one million pilgrims come yearly to wash away their sins in the holy Ganges, I would bump into Ravi. As it was, Ravi was fresh in town, visiting his family, and was renting a boat to take his sister out for a sunset paddle. Without missing a beat, I jumped in, and we were rowing on the Ganges River with the orange sun sinking into the horizon.

At this point of my story, Cha Chi was in disbelief. 'Only in India is this possible' the saying goes. How can such unplanned meetings occur effortlessly? These and other such events have challenged my beliefs and altered my life in ways previously unthinkable.

Chapter Nine

Our lives are connected by a thousand invisible threads.

Herman Melville

The Ritz Carlton
Vicki Michaels

In October, 1976, Joe had taken me for a very lovely dinner at the Ritz Carlton. As usual upon leaving, he needed to use the men's room. It was a long hike to where he needed to go, so I was amusing myself looking at all the expensive and gorgeous things they have for sale in their vitrines.

I was thinking no evil when, as three men were breezing past me one of them said, sotto voce: "That's exactly the kind of girl Joe Michaels would go for!" By the time my head stopped spinning, they were halfway down the "football field" to the men's room. I followed them. When Joe came out of the men's room, I told him what I'd overheard. He went back into the men's.

As it turned out, the three men were friends that Joe had not seen since 1950: Miles, Lowell, and Buddie. After graduating from college in 1949, the four of them traveled together in Europe. One man had been Joe's roommate in college. Another, who lived in New York, had gone from kindergarten through high school with him.

We all went for a drink, and the fellows caught up on their lives. Joe continued to stay in touch with them until he died.

Family Reunion
Bobbi Zehner

As the Amtrak train pulled into St. Cloud, Minnesota, I was awakened by the sounds of people boarding the area around me. It was one o'clock in the morning; the beginning of a three-week journey to Seattle, San Francisco, down to Los Angeles and back home to Madison, Wisconsin. Sneaking a peek at the new arrivals, I noticed five adults and two children: some whispering, others signing. As an educational sign language interpreter, alone on the second day of summer vacation, it occurred to me that by breakfast I might have a new friend or two.

And so it was that I made the acquaintance of Kevin, an inquisitive five-year-old, originally from Korea. Kevin had been adopted the year before and was excited about being able to communicate with a total stranger as he traveled across country with his new family. While he was a congenial little fellow, I was grateful to have Lionel Richie and The Commodores on a cassette player by my side. Because every time I glanced up, there perched Kevin over the back of his seat, patiently waiting to pounce. "You sleeping?" he would sign eagerly. Sometimes I would offer a concurring nod and just close my eyes. But not so often that I missed this charming lad's personal story.

Kevin's adoptive mother was accompanied by her two adult children and their spouses. Like Kevin, her adult son was deaf, as was the daughter's husband. Both mother and daughter were sign language interpreters in their home school district, so we had something in common. The group was traveling to a family reunion in Montana.

Two years earlier, when the mother decided to adopt a child, she specified that she wanted a deaf child. During the agency's search, Kevin's name popped up. So successfully did he join this family that a year later the mother applied to adopt a second child. And as serendipity would have it, the agency found another Korean child, a girl a little older than Kevin, who was also deaf. It sounded so right.

When Kevin and his family went to the airport to meet his new sister, they discovered just how right, as the two youngsters tearfully rushed into each other's arms. They knew what no one else knew: they were natural siblings, separated at the orphanage when Kevin came to the United States. Siblings, who never expected to see each other ever again.

It did not occur to the adoption agency that Kevin might have left a sister behind, as such is not the practice in the States. Now when I think about family reunions, this one stands apart: the one which helped make my solo train trip a unique and heartfelt experience.

I Miss Your Amazing Smile
Neil Amber

Life is a profound journey, whether lived consciously as an adventure, or as a struggle with a series of obligations and rote tasks. Life can be about looking only after ourselves, or it can be a service to others. Whether in a family or as a loner, whether wealthy or a pauper, we all meet the same destination. We all must eventually shed our skin and bones and become mere, yet marvellous, memory.

I was half-awake in the middle of the night, couldn't sleep. Watching images of water flowing. Thoughts of Sam's ashes dispersing into the Ganges River, flowing here and there, delayed in some eddies, then flowing on towards the Bay of Bengal. Memories of my times with him appeared: from spending hours looking for him in the parking lot after a Led Zeppelin concert in our teens, to our epic travels in the mountains of Yunnan as guys in our mid 50's. The memories all blended together, appeared and disappeared. What stayed with me most was Sam Mitchell's amazing smile.

I then reflected on the cremations I'd watched in Varanasi (Benares) years ago during a winter solstice. Many people believe their karma is transformed if they are cremated along the Ganges. So this is what Sam was up to, one of the thousands who come each year to Benares to die. Perhaps these words of Kabir, a mystic poet from Benares, were on Sam's lips in his last moments:

My heart is frenzied, and I disclose in my soul what is hidden.
I am immersed in that one great bliss which transcends
all pleasure and pain. ...

While attending Hindu University in this very ancient city of Varanasi, Sam's Ph.D. dissertation had focused on Kabir. Sam was a lover of life's mystery, so Kabir was the perfect man for him to emulate. Kabir in Arabic means 'the great'; he was the first saint to harmonize Hindu and

Islamic teachings and to show a path these two religions could tread together. Kabir was a true weaver both of cloth and of unity.

Sam and I had been out of touch for some years. Yet, as I would discover, the curious vagabond in each of us would draw us together. My partner Karla and I had spent the day at a beach in south Kerala (India) and were about to take the bus back to our hotel. Instead, we decided to have a cup of Chai at a tea stall in the coconut groves and watch the sun set into the Arabian Sea. As we turned around, I was startled to see Sam and his amazing smile. Sam, a lover of Hindi films, had just gotten off a 40-hour train trip from Varanasi for a Hindi film festival in Trivandrum. This meeting was unplanned and incredible. We spent a few days together. And we talked, and we connected, and we talked even more. Sam contended that his life direction had been largely influenced by a slide show I'd presented in our hometown about my first travels to India.

We agreed to stay in contact. I visited him in Honolulu while he was completing his Asian studies program and met his Chinese girlfriend, Yuan, whom he soon married. They visited us in our first home in California and years later in our home here in Wilsons Creek (Australia). A few years later, I discovered I had ample mileage to fly all the way to Kunming. It was to be epic, time off and—yes, what I loved, adventure--for five weeks. Sam, with his amazing smile, was at the airport to greet me.

We walked through the stone forest maze, explored old Taoist temples in a hilly forest, and hiked in the tiger-leaping gorge above the Yangtze River. On our road trip, Sam and I shared very raw emotions, from experiencing immense joy to visiting our pain and deepest longings. Often our mood fit an old Led Zeppelin song:
'And as we wind on down the road, our shadows taller than our soul'
This spoke volumes about Sam's sadness, his subterranean world, which that amazing smile often disguised.

Upon my departure, I was gifted green tea from Pu're, and he was insistent that I learn to pronounce the famous tea region correctly. I often couldn't tell if he was being serious or just not neglecting important nuances. What would become a fact only later, as I said thank you with a warm hug, was this would be the final time I'd take in Sam's amazing smile. I miss you, brother.

Parallel Lives
Kathy Farrell, as told to Kate Conklin Corcoran

At a Wisconsin get-together party in Denton, Texas, Kathy Farrell was introduced to a woman, Jane, whom she should have met many years before. The two have lived parallel lives, in the same neighborhoods, but never knew of the other's existence until this party.
In Denton, Kathy and Jane live one block apart.

❖ When the Farrells lived on Colorado Avenue in Sun Prairie, Wisconsin, Jane and her family lived only two blocks away.

❖ The Farrells moved to a second house in Sun Prairie; Jane and her family moved one block from that house.

❖ Cailin Farrell's babysitter bought that second house from Jane's family.

❖ Both Kathy's and Jane's daughters were on the Pom Squad at Sun Prairie High School, though Jane's daughter was four years younger than Cailin Farrell.

❖ Both daughters, each an only child, moved to Dallas as young adults.

❖ Both sets of parents moved to Denton in retirement to be near their daughters.

College Choices
Anne Lundin

Planning to be a glorified secretary, I was a senior in high school in 1962, living in Ridgewood, New Jersey, a suburb of New York City. Because my mother had once been an executive secretary in the big city, she had groomed my expectations so that I thought of going to a junior college and then transferring to a 4-year school if my glamour job never appeared. My father, on the other hand, had higher aspirations and urged me to go directly to a 4-year college. It was late in the senior year to be making changes, but I decided he might be right and also wondered how successful I would ever be as a secretary anyway, never having mastered touch typing in my high school typing class.

The question arose: where would I go? My father, a Presbyterian minister, was keen on a church-related school. Wooster College in Ohio came to mind since my uncle Jack, my mother's brother, had once been a faculty member. Since we were heading to Ohio, I thought also of Ohio Wesleyan. I had gone out on a date with someone who had been a student there and liked it--and it was Methodist. I didn't do any research, just acted on a whim.

My mother, who rarely called her brother, communicated to him our intentions for this trip to Wooster and Wesleyan. He mentioned that my mother's old boyfriend from the 1930s was still on the faculty at Ohio Wesleyan. They knew each other slightly through shared academic interests in philosophy and religion. My uncle suggested she call him when we got to campus to say hello and perhaps learn more about the school.

We first went to Wooster, where it was very quiet (spring break). To the studious young man showing us around a staid, hohum-looking campus, I asked, "What do students do on a Saturday night?" That was important to me.

He replied, "Oh, we usually go to the library." Well, not I, I thought as we were soon on the road to Delaware, Ohio, the small college town where Ohio Wesleyan was located and where my hopes for weekends lay. Here we had a more spirited tour. And my mother called her old boyfriend, Loyd Easton, Professor of Philosophy, who invited us to stop by. Timing-wise, it was awkward. He was recently widowed and had three school-age children there at the house, but we made our greetings, a contact indeed propitious.

There was clearly to my eyes (and theirs) a spark between my mother and her old beau. Yes, indeed. He had courted her in the 1930s when both lived in New York City, but left her for another whom he married, after which she married my father, hastily, regretfully. Loyd

Easton was clearly interested in my mother and supportive of me, especially when I decided then and there to attend Wesleyan. Then I showed up not too many months later for freshman camp. He took a keen interest in my welfare and my mother's. At various times during this year he saw her, and they wrote and called on a regular basis.

Finally, by Thanksgiving of my sophomore year, they were married. My college town became my new hometown, my mother gained a good man, and I a good step-father. They married in 1963 and had a long second marriage of 37 years, ending with his death in 2000. It wasn't always easy with a blended family that resisted blending, but it essentially worked. They were happy together, loved long.

I have often thought of the quirkiness by which I chose a college and how congruent that became for my mother's life, for my life. My mother garnered the courage to leave her miserable marriage and to do something adventurous, risky. She gained a secure relationship and a small college town in which to thrive as a faculty wife. For me, I gained footing as well. My stepfather, unlike my critical, distant father, believed in me strongly, thinking I could do anything. I later did, becoming a professor and, alas, never the secretary. Thanks be to those guardian intuitive spirits, the angels of serendipity.

A Map to Mirror Lake
Kate Conklin Corcoran

Since 1982, members of my extended family have participated in an annual camping trip. For most of our trips, we chose Wisconsin state parks, even though most of the campers were from the Chicago area. Wisconsin State Parks are beautifully maintained, inexpensive, and plentiful enough to have many choices within a three-hour ride of Chicago. My mother, sisters, and brothers attended virtually every year. Some years, cousins, aunts, even our great-aunt joined us. Two of the most faithful members of the Conklin Family Camping Trip were my aunt and uncle, Mary Pat and Gene Fontaine.

Mary Pat and Gene were two of the inexhaustible hikers in the family. Most years, they had barely unpacked before they were off walking, and they hiked every day. They had great sense of direction and great stamina—until one hike at Mirror Lake. Although they remembered the number of the campsite, they were lost and wandering in circles, unable to get back to the campground. Then they saw, lying in the grass, a map of the campground—with their number of the campsite circled. Somehow, someone in our group, or a previous camper at that site, had lost that map. Did someone drop it on their own walk? Did it blow out of a car window? Wherever it had come from, it helped Mary Pat and Gene find their way back.

From Idaho to Italy
Jayne Collins

In the spring of 2001, I met a woman named Maria, who walked into my real estate office one day. I ended up selling her a darling 1900-era house I had long admired.

We'd become friendly while working together. She was planning to have her elderly mother live with her. Maria was soon retiring after many years teaching Romance languages at various universities. That was all I knew about her personal life.

A couple of months later I was off on a three-week trip around Italy. After starting with a week at a villa in Tuscany, I spent some time exploring the Florence area. In the last week, I traveled to the Italian Riviera, stopping along coastal towns whenever they appealed to me. Just before Portofino, I found a gorgeous harbor town called Santa Margherita, which I absolutely loved.

After getting settled into a beautiful five-story hotel near the water, I walked out on the terrace. A few people were enjoying the view late in the afternoon, the water was a dark turquoise, and there wasn't a cloud in the sky. "I love Italy," I remember thinking...it was perfect. I started chatting with a young couple from Florida. They asked where I was from, and I said Idaho. They said it was strange that earlier that day, while on a train traveling up the coast, there had been a group of Americans from a university in Idaho.

A few moments later, two casually-dressed men walked out onto the terrace with a bottle of wine and sat down a few yards away from us. The Florida couple looked at me and said, "Those are two of the guys from the Idaho group from the train!" I had to check it out, so I wandered over to their table.

Soon I was sitting down with the two of them discussing Idaho. They were from Moscow, in northern Idaho, and worked for the University of Idaho. They were on a tour through Italy with a group of students. When I mentioned that I was from Boise, one of the guys asked if I knew of Pengilly's Bar downtown.

"Of course I do," I said, "An old friend of mine is a regular there; he has his own personal stool at the bar!"

The man looked at me and asked, "Who?" When I said "George", he responded, "George was the best man in my wedding 23 years ago!"

Well, after that, we kept the wine flowing and some of the U of I students came outside to join us. When they made dinner plans at a nearby restaurant, they invited me to join them. It was like having our own private Idaho dinner party, all of us talking and enjoying being together in Italy!

I sat next to a very nice student, Alissa. As we visited over dinner, I asked how she happened to be on this trip. She told me that her language teacher, whom she'd grown very close to, had suggested the trip, as she was going to be one of the staff accompanying the group. Alissa also mentioned that her teacher had recently bought a home in Boise and had settled in with her elderly mother before leaving on the trip.

I felt moved to ask her, "What is your teacher's name?"

When she replied, "Maria _____ ", I realized that she was my Boise real estate client. Wow--what are the chances!

It turned out that Maria was with some of the other students, at that very moment, in Turin. The group I was having dinner with that evening was heading back to Turin by train in a few days. I asked Alissa to surprise Maria with a hello from her Boise realtor... currently vacationing in Santa Margherita!   What a wonderful way to end a wonderful evening on the coast of Italy.

Ex-pats in Winter Park
Bobbi Zehner

Over the years, as I have collected other people's stories of synchronicity, I continue to be amazed that some of my own stories remain unplumbed--until someone's tale strikes a familiar chord. The sharing of old memories and new old memories seems a limitless joy for many.

For example, when Jayne Collins contacted me about a story she thought might suit *Under a Shared Umbrella,* one of her questions was: "Have you ever been to Durango, Colorado?"   After a pause for reflection, a sudden flash of memory led me to write back to her:

"When you asked me if I had ever been to Durango, Jayne, it triggered the remembrance of a road trip from San Francisco to Chicago with a former sweetheart, Rae Welch. We decided to stop for dinner at a Best Western in Colorado. When I first saw the Winter Park exit sign, I remembered that my buddy Billy Finnegan had left Chicago for Winter Park, but I had no idea if he was still there or where there might be. When we walked into the Best Western, I was greeted by a grinning bartender, who said, 'Well, well, well, look at who's here!'

"No, it was not Billy. It was Dave Zwicker, another Chicago friend. I didn't know that Dave had left Chicago, much less for Winter Park, or that he even knew Finnegan. Knew him? They were roommates. Dave led us to their place for an impromptu party with Billy and a few other Chicago ex-pats. We stayed up most the night, Rae playing his guitar, and the rest of us butchering some otherwise lovely tunes.

"'Thanks for bringing it back to me like it was yesterday, Jayne.'"

Chapter Ten

Every person is a new door to a different world.

David Mamet, *Six Degrees of Separation*

Airport Providence
Sheila Waldman

It was 5:30 a.m. on October 1st, 2001, two weeks after the 9/11 attacks in NYC. I was traveling to St. Louis, MO. Because of the tragedy, it was necessary for travelers to be to the airport well in advance of their flights. I was walking up to the security line when a very handsome man caught my attention. Our eyes met, we exchanged smiles, but I had to go to the back of the line and he was at least 100 people ahead of me. In an international airport, given the countless flights leaving every minute, I knew I was not going to see him again. For all I knew, he didn't even speak English, or he lived across the country and was just traveling through

I proceeded through the security line. At my gate, I realized that there was not a CNN TV monitor in the waiting area. I had been glued to the TV since 9/11 and wanted to stay tuned in, especially while at the airport. So I moved down several gates until I found a CNN monitor turned on. Knowing that my plane was not leaving for over an hour, I settled in.

A few minutes later, that same handsome man I saw in the security line walked to his gate: the gate where I, by chance, had decided to sit. There was an open seat next to me, and he came over. This time we did more than exchange glances. I learned that his name was Brett Waldman. He did speak English. He lived in Minneapolis, where I already had been living for fifteen years, and was traveling to Milwaukee on business for the day. Long story short, two days later we had our first date, and knew we had found our soul mates. Thirteen months later we were married. Almost ten years later, we joyfully work and play together every day.

We know that if either of us would have been delayed by a stoplight or taken a different way to the airport that day, we may never have met. We were literally in the right place at exactly the right moment. We know that God had a plan for us as individuals and as a couple. We are grateful every day for the gift of love and companionship that the One Above gave to us.

When Vietnam Vets Connect
Elaine Kelly

A short story of synchronicity: We recently had some upgrades installed in our bathroom. Marty, the technician from Re-Bath, had shown interest in Dennis's being a Vietnam veteran. Marty shared that he meets returning veterans at the airport when they are coming home. An old softy, Dennis is always touched when folks honor vets and treat them well; he wasn't always treated well himself. The next day, Marty shared the following story with me.

Marty's father was sent to fight in Vietnam. When he returned from the war, he had problems with substance abuse and was psychologically damaged. He abused Marty's mother repeatedly, and she finally divorced him. She remarried. Her second husband raised Marty like his own son, and Marty thought of his stepfather as his father.

Marty's stepfather died last Thanksgiving. Shortly thereafter, Marty received a call from somebody purporting to be his father. Marty responded, "Is this some kind of sick joke? My father just died!"

Turns out, it was Marty's biological father. The father was being treated at the local VA Hospital. He mentioned to his nurse that he had been trying to connect with his estranged son, whom he hadn't seen or contacted since the divorce. But Marty wasn't listed in the phone book. Amazingly, the nurse recognized Marty's name. She told the father that Marty worked for Re-Bath and had recently done work in her own home. She had Marty's work cell phone number and gave it to the father. The father then called Marty.

A happy ending: Marty and his sister are getting to know their biological father better and are now including him in family celebrations. What a blessing!

35 Hillbrow
Vicki Michaels

When I was working at Playboy in Chicago, there was a copywriter named Elaine. A very glamorous blonde in her late thirties or forties who always wore large hats. She was lovely. We were chatting one day when she mentioned her brother lived in London, where I grew up. My parents separated when I was twelve. They didn't just separate. My mother told me after dinner one night they were going to divorce; that Daddy and she had found separate apartments, and we were leaving 35 Hillbrow the next morning.

While talking with Elaine about London, she casually mentioned where her brother had lived: 35 Hillbrow. The exact apartment where I grew up! The importance of his living in that apartment was that it had been such a devastating experience for me: having home and parents one day but not the next. And then so very many years later to learn it was being lived in by happy people who loved it.

Fast forward to 2000. My husband Joe had taken our son Gregory and Joe's granddaughter and her friend to Belgium. Gregory was to spend two weeks with friends of ours in France. I arranged to fly into Paris, so that Joe and I could drive Greg to Deauville the next day. The night before my flight, I got a call. Joe had had a stroke. It was the same day the Concorde crashed in Paris. I couldn't get there any earlier than my planned flight. Didn't even know if I would be able to land.

When I finally arrived in Paris, I put Greg and Joe to bed and went for a much-needed cocktail in the hotel lounge. I sat down next to an American businessman. As we chatted, I discovered that he was living in London. Guess where? 35 Hillbrow!

Thai Hospitality
Bobbi Zehner

Because Thailand doesn't have an educational system capable of addressing her son's needs, Sangrawee and Pedos moved to Madison, where she enrolled him in La Follette's Special Ed program. There, I teach Pedos sign language, serve as his classroom interpreter and bond with him in ways common to those of us working one-to-one with students. During their second year in Wisconsin, Sangrawee invites me to spend the winter break in Thailand: an invitation I relish until mid-flight over the North Atlantic, when an uneasy feeling starts to grow.

Dong, Pedos' father, is a surgeon and has remained in Bangkok as the chief of a private hospital. We are on our way to visit Dong and their extended family over what becomes our extended stay. It is January of 1996, and the U.S. Government has completely shut down. On a companion ticket with a Thai national, I will not be flying home as early as planned.

Today, in 2012, while reading my journal entries from Thailand, I realize that I cannot give the scope of that adventure justice in its retelling. However, I can share two forgotten brief encounters tucked into the pages of that journal. And wonder, yet again, at the synchronicity of life.

On Christmas Eve, in 1995, my brother Jimmy tunes the television to a PBS special about Father Brennan, the Chicago priest who had started an orphanage and school for the deaf in Thailand. Jim says, "You should visit that school in Pattaya, Bobbi."

"How about that. One of my side trips will be to Pattaya. I'll definitely keep it in mind." And as luck would have it, I did make a visit to Father Brennan, who introduced me to Chomchan, a 32-year-old teacher. She had never met an American before, much less one who used sign language. We communicated as if we were old friends.

Chomchan then introduced me to a hearing woman, who led me on a tour of the nurseries. Her English was impeccable and I told her so. "That's because I'm an Australian," beamed a face with beautiful Asian features. We shared the kind of laugh I suspect she has shared before.

A week later, back in Bangkok, I was waiting on the street for a store to open. Several others were also waiting, when I did a double-take. Ranie, the English-speaking woman from the orphanage, was grinning like we were old friends. Five million people in Bangkok, and this American bumps into the Australian I first met in Pattaya, two hours away.

Add this to that skootchie "small world" story: while later waiting in the Tokyo airport for the second leg of my trip home, I took a seat wherever I could find one. My gate was SRO and I had time to kill, so I planted myself at another gate and focused mostly on journaling. After an hour, the woman sitting next to me said, "Excuse me, I need to catch my flight to Chicago."

"Do you live in Chicago?"

"No, I live in Madison."

"I'm connecting in Minneapolis, but I live in Madison!"

She was returning from a trip to China and we should not have been sitting side-by-side, waiting to board flights departing to different destinations. She lives on Whitney Way, five minutes from my home. We were both struck by the "what-ifs" of the moment and marveled at the workings of the universe. So much for six degrees of separation.

A Postcard to My Sister
Jayne Collins

Some amazing connections occurred while I was living in Lisbon, Portugal. Considering I had never been there, nor did I speak a word of Portuguese when I arrived, I certainly didn't know what to expect in my new world--except for something very different than what I'd been used to. You see, I'd become fed up with my somewhat mundane life in Durango, Colorado for the past eight years—and I had been a real estate broker for sixteen years. I knew one thing for sure: it was time to shake things up.

After the real estate crash of 2008, home sales came to a screeching halt, and that was just the push I needed to follow my heart. I'd lived in many beautiful places in the US, from Hawaii to New Mexico and almost every Rocky Mountain state in between. I was ready for a cultural change this time.

After a three-week trip around northern Italy in 2001, I decided that I wanted to spend more time in Europe, and not as a tourist. My goal became moving to Europe and having a real life there. It took me until 2009 to make it happen, and Portugal became my destination.

I prepared to become an English teacher in Portugal and was ready for an adventure!

I first flew to Madrid, Spain and spent five days there before making my way by train and bus to Portugal in the gorgeous sunny, warm September weather.

That winter, I sent my youngest sister Andrea a postcard. She brought it to work, a large law firm in the Detroit area. She taped it to her computer, which was unusual for her to do--she didn't normally receive postcards or tape things to her computer. One day an attorney saw the postcard and asked her about it. Andrea replied, "My sister Jayne is living in Lisbon; she sent it to me."

Libby, the attorney, responded with, "Well, that's funny because my sister Nancy lives in Porto. She's a violinist and has lived there for 20 years. We should get them together!" Andrea agreed, so each of them emailed us the other's contact information, with an explanation attached.

A week later, my cell phone rang and it was Nancy calling from Porto! When we had chatted a while, she informed me that The Orchestra of Portugal, for which she played violin, would be playing a concert in Lisbon soon. Did I want to come? I said yes, and she gave me the specifics and said there would be a ticket waiting for me at the box office. Afterward, we would all have drinks at the hotel where they'd be staying the night. I was happy to be making plans for a fun evening with a new friend and group of international musicians, too. It sounded like a perfect evening!

And so, on the following Saturday, I made my way to the huge, gorgeous concert hall, picked up my free ticket at the box office, and enjoyed the wonderful music they created.

Afterward, I met Nancy in front of the tour bus, as we'd arranged, and we hugged each other and chatted like old friends. As we boarded the tour bus, she introduced me to each musician. There were quite a few of them, and they were from all over the world, including a couple of Americans. I found this rather surprising, and was looking forward to relaxing at the hotel bar so we could all talk comfortably and get to know each other a bit.

After unloading from the bus, the musicians quickly checked into their rooms and then reconvened at the large open-style bar. We all ordered drinks and started moving tables together. As the cocktails started flowing, the musicians visibly relaxed into their chairs and couches, smiles on all their faces as they conversed easily with each other. I was amazed at hearing so much English being spoken in one place. It was such a rare occurrence in Lisbon, I realized. I felt happy and relaxed, too, and ready to compare stories with my new acquaintances.

Shortly after I chose a seat amongst the musicians, John, a tall, 50-ish man, plopped down next to me with a grin on his face and said hello in an American accent. He had an easy, relaxed manner about him, so we started talking comfortably with each other right away.

I had noticed him on stage during the concert; he was being showcased as a special guest who was touring with the orchestra. Apparently, he was a well-known American jazz drummer, and he was very good, but I'd never heard of him before. We continued our conversation about what we were doing in Portugal and our impressions of it. I started remembering another jazz drummer I'd met while living in Santa Fe, New Mexico in the mid-1980s. I had worked at the only real nightclub in town back then, and we had the best live music around.

I had met Danny when he was on tour with a very well-known band (Al DiMeola), and they'd played at the club. We had talked before and after the show. He had even walked me to my car, and then he'd invited me to come down to the next show in Albuquerque. I ended up going to that show, too, and he sent for me to come backstage and hang out in the "green room". As he and I sat talking on a couch, a few people came up and asked him for his autograph. He was very cool and casual about it, like it was no big deal at all. He seemed like a truly sweet and talented guy, but the band was on its way to the next stop. Danny gave me his phone number and told me to call if I ever went to New York City.

I mentioned this to John and asked him if he happened to know Danny Gottlieb. His mouth fell open, and he just stared at me for a moment, in shock. He then replied, "Danny is a really good friend of mine; he and I grew up next to each other in New Jersey. Then we both lived in New York, and now he's living in Florida. As a matter of fact, he just called me a week or so ago and left me a message." John started scrolling thru his phone until he found the message--then he grinned and said, "I think I'll send him a text and see if he's still up!" A couple of minutes later, his phone made a dinging noise. He read the message and looked at me. "He's up and I think we should call him!" So he did, and after they chatted for a bit, John told him, "Hey Danny, I'm sitting here with a bunch of musicians and this American gal who is friends with the violinist. She just told me that you two met back in 1986 at a nightclub in Santa Fe. Do you remember her?" Danny must have said yes, because John handed me his cell phone, and after 25 years, Danny and I had a wonderful conversation.

It was actually really nice catching up with him after so long, and he sounded good. I did tease him a bit when I said, "Who knew your name would come up between two Americans in a hotel bar at one a.m. in Lisbon, Portugal?"

It just goes to show that you never know who you might meet, wherever you are in the world. Once people start a conversation, the most surprising coincidences can appear and give you a good story to share down the road of life.

A Case of Mistaken Identity
Carol Schoenherr

I attended the University of Wisconsin-Madison for two years and then transferred to UW-Milwaukee. I really knew only one other person going to Milwaukee, an acquaintance, Nancy, who was going into nursing.

On my first day, my first class was Psychology. As I was walking there, I saw a girl walking toward me, whom I thought I recognized as Nancy and assumed she was going to the Nursing Building. As fate would have it, the Nursing Building was right next to the Psychology Building.

I said, "Hi, Nancy."

She said, "I'm not Nancy. I'm Kay. Do you happen to know where the Psychology Building is?"

I said, "I'm going there right now."

Turns out, we were in the same class, sat together and our friendship grew from there. I was unhappy with my roommate and there was a vacancy in Kay's suite. I moved in. Although we only knew each other for a short while, it was an important relationship that started with a case of mistaken identity.

Major Phil Seep
Marsh Olech

When I was in the Navy, my best friend was Major Phil Seep, the commandant of the Marine detachment on the USS Constellation. A Korean War vet, he went back in the service when Vietnam erupted. He was a bit older than me, so he showed me the ropes in the Philippines, Vietnam, and Japan. When we returned to port in San Diego, we embarked on a series of adventures and road trips.

When I left the Navy, he gave me a lot of surplus gear to take with me. Years later, I always wondered what happened to him. I even tried to locate him through Marine directories, without luck. I remembered that he was from Wisconsin and had an ex-wife and five kids there.

About seven years ago, a friend of mine, Howard Williamson, retired and bought an old farm near the Wisconsin Dells. Occasionally, I would visit there from Chicago. One time he was showing me the Veterans Memorial. I looked to the side, and there was a plaque to the memory of Major Phil Seep.

I said, "This was my friend. I have looked for him for years."

Howard said, "There are a lot of the Seep family here. I will look into it."

Three weeks later, Howard met a Pat Seep and told him about my search for Phil. Pat was Phil's brother, and he definitely wanted to meet me. Phil had died of a heart attack a few years prior. The next time I visited, I brought pictures I had taken of Phil in the service. Pat and the rest of his brothers, five of them all now in their 70s, came to Howard's house. We had a great time telling war stories. The next year they had a family reunion and invited me. There I met Phil's sister and one of his sons. I'm sure Phil was smiling down.

Canadian Inspirations
Liz Gillette

Twenty-eight years ago, I left Canada with my two children to live back in New Zealand. Whilst I was living in Canada, I did some hairdressing from my home. As I left Canada in a hurry without telling a soul (that's another story), I was unable to contact my clients.

Jump ahead to eight years ago. I was working in Auckland in a real estate office. On one beautiful summer's day, I saw a couple looking at pictures in the window. I wandered out to see if I could help them, but they told me they were just in New Zealand on a holiday. I asked where they were from, and they said "Canada." I replied that I had lived in Calgary. They also came from Calgary. When I told them which suburb I had lived in, the woman shrieked and said, "Oh my god. It's Liz! You used to do my hair. It's me—Sue Blair!" With that, we both hugged and shed tears of joy; we were like two school kids with excitement.

Sue went on to tell me that five minutes before she had walked past a beauty salon and said to her husband, "I wonder what ever happened to Liz who used to do my hair." And then, around the corner, there I was!

As we further renewed our acquaintance, Sue and John told me they had moved to Vancouver Island, bought a 38-foot sloop, and sailed to New Zealand. As we talked, we rekindled our friendship. In August this year, I flew to Vancouver where my daughter and ten-year-old granddaughter met me. We sailed around Vancouver Island for four glorious days with Sue and John on *Tamarac 11*. Sue has now written a book called *Waiting for the Moon*. This amazing couple is an inspiration.

Reconnected
Kate Conklin Corcoran

Tom Sparrow had only joined the Friendster social network because his friend Eric had begged him: "I don't have any friends online!" Tom signed up and posted his personal information, but he rarely checked the site after that initial posting. Because he didn't want to use Friendster to communicate, he had requested email messages only. In July 2006, he noticed a message from a Zaianne Kuhiri: "Are you the same Tom Sparrow from my second grade class?"

Not really recognizing the name Zaianne, Tom waited several months before replying. "If you went to Jefferson Elementary in DeKalb, Illinois around 1990, then yes."

He received a very quick response. "Do you remember a little Malaysian girl in your class? That was me."

Tom did somewhat remember who she was, though he didn't recall speaking to her very much, if at all. While they had been in the same classrooms for grades 2-4, they had not been friends, although they did have friends in common. Zaianne's mother had been earning her master's degree at Northern Illinois University, but the family moved back to Malaysia after those three years. In a photo taken just before the family's departure, Tom is in the background. Zaianne has said people looking at the photo often asked her who was that boy.

When Zaianne first contacted Tom, she was, in fact, in Kuala Lumpur visiting her family. But she was a full-time student at New York University, in an Interactive Telecommunications Program, majoring in animation and game design. Beyond the grade school connection, they discovered another connection as they communicated. Tom had just completed his degree at the Illinois Institute of Art—also specializing in animation and game design.

Once Zaianne returned from Malaysia to New York to complete her degree, she continued to email Tom occasionally.

Following some impulse, on Christmas Eve 2006, Tom decided to telephone all of the friends he had not talked to in a while. After going through his entire phone list, he decided to place a call to Zaianne, too—the first time they actually spoke. To Tom, Zaianne sounded "sweet, cute." Almost giddy, Zaianne confided to her roommate that Tom "sounded really cute." She had remembered the little Tommy Sparrow with the squeaky high voice. Once she heard his "adult" voice, Zaianne's image of him changed.

As they continued their telephone and online communications, Tom and Zaianne decided that they liked each other enough to meet face-to-face. Zaianne had already planned to attend the 2007 Annual Malaysian Midwest Games—held that year in DeKalb, Illinois: Tom's home town. In June, Tom flew to New York. And in August, to celebrate Tom's 25th birthday, they traveled together to Las Vegas.

Zaianne, with her master's degree completed and a wide variety of job opportunities, made the decision to move to the Chicago area, to see where this relationship might lead. It led to their marriage, on July 26, 2008.

Author Biographies

A retired English teacher, Kate Conklin Corcoran is an avid reader, writer, and editor. She has always been fascinated by the life stories of other people and the way books share those life stories. Following a thirty-year career as an English teacher in the Madison public schools, she now works a program associate at the University of Wisconsin-Madison. She lives with her husband and two grandsons in Madison, Wisconsin.

Bobbi Zehner's sense of curiosity has led her to uncover "small world" stories similar to her own. As she continues to write her tales and collect those of others, the inevitable is happening: a desire to share those tales as an anthology. Bobbi, California-born and Chicago-bred, is a former high school sign language interpreter in Madison, Wisconsin, where she met up with Kate Conklin, another Chicago ex-pat. Since then, the two have become great friends with a mutual commitment to collecting "feel good" stories.

We are continuing to collect stories of synchronicity. If you have a tale to share, please contact us at: bobbiz@sbcglobal.net or kathleen_conklin@msn.com.

Made in the USA
Columbia, SC
02 April 2021